EXPLORATIONS IN LO

REGIONAL HIST(

Centre for English Local History, University of Leicester
and
Centre for Regional and Local History, University of Hertfordshire

SERIES EDITORS: HAROLD FOX AND NIGEL GOOSE

Previous title in this series

Volume 1: *Landscapes Decoded: the origins and development of Cambridgeshire's medieval fields*
by SUSAN OOSTHUIZEN
(ISBN 978-1-902806-58-7)

THE SELF-CONTAINED VILLAGE?

The social history of rural communities, 1250–1900

EDITED BY CHRISTOPHER DYER

UNIVERSITY OF HERTFORDSHIRE PRESS

Explorations in Local and Regional History

Volume 2

First published in Great Britain in 2007 by
University of Hertfordshire Press
Learning and Information Services
University of Hertfordshire
College Lane
Hatfield
Hertfordshire AL10 9AB

British Library Cataloguing in Publication Data
A catalogue record for this book is available from the British Library

ISBN 978-1-902806-59-4

Design by Geoff Green Book Design, CB4 5RA
Cover design by John Robertshaw, AL5 2JB
Printed in Great Britain by Antony Rowe Ltd, SN14 6LH

Contents

Figures

Tables

Contributors

David Brown is a freelance historian. Having completed a thesis on enclosure at the University of Wolverhampton, his book, 'An Honest, Industrious and Useful Description of People': Itinerant Retailing and its Role in the Economy 1600–1900, will soon be published.

Christopher Dyer, Professor of Regional and Local History, University of Leicester, has published on a number of aspects of the countryside and towns in the Middle Ages. His most recent book is An Age of Transition? Economy and Society in England in the Later Middle Ages (2005).

Henry French, Lecturer in History, University of Exeter, has worked on early modern rural society with Professor Richard Hoyle, and is joint author of The Character of English Rural Society 1550–1750: Earls Colne Revisited (2006), and is currently preparing a book on the Middle Sort of People.

Steve Hindle, Professor of History, University of Warwick, has written extensively on rural society and government, most recently in On the Parish? The Micro-Politics of Poor Relief in Rural England, c. 1550–1750 (2004).

Jane Whittle, Senior Lecturer in History, University of Exeter, works on late medieval and early modern society and economy, most recently on consumption and women's work. Her book The Development of Agrarian Capitalism: Land and Labour in Norfolk 1440–1580 appeared in 2000.

Ian Whyte, Professor of Historical Geography, University of Lancaster, has published widely on Scottish historical geography and social and economic history. He is currently working on landscape and socio-economic change in the uplands of north-west England. Recent books include Transforming Fell and Valley: Landscape and Parliamentary Enclosure in North-West England (2003) and Society, Landscape and Environment in Upland Britain (2005), edited with A. Winchester.

Series Editors' Preface

This new series of *Explorations in Local and Regional History* is a continuation and development of the 'Occasional Papers' of the University of Leicester's Department of English Local History, a series started by Herbert Finberg in 1952.[1] Appropriately, the new series is published by the University of Hertfordshire Press, which has a strong and growing profile in English local and regional history. The Occasional Papers were described by Maurice Beresford, in a review, as 'the glory of Leicester University Press' and in Finberg's *Times* obituary as his 'brilliant series'. One can see why, for many of them introduced themes and methods which were new when they appeared, and which have been followed up and imitated in much subsequent work. Such was Alan Everitt's monograph on Kent in the Civil War, Finberg's own on continuity between Roman and Saxon settlement in the Cotswolds, David Hey's on rural by-employment, Charles Phythian-Adams' on early estates and their fission, Christopher Dyer's on the parish of Hanbury and Keith Snell's on the 1851 religious census. Many of the Occasional Papers did not sell well, for they were short in length – around 15–20,000 words or even fewer – and booksellers despaired of the fact that they had no spine, which meant they did not display well. A new, more substantial, series was started in 2001, but the publisher ceased operations almost immediately after the publication of the first volume and the series lapsed until its adoption by the University of Hertfordshire Press.

Explorations in Local and Regional History will have three distinctive characteristics. First, the series will be prepared to publish work on novel themes, to tackle fresh subjects – perhaps even unusual ones. We hope that it will serve to open up new approaches, prompt the analysis of new sources or types of source, and foster new methodologies. This is not to suggest that more traditional scholarship in local and regional history will be unrepresented, for it may well be

---

1.   The Occasional Papers and related publications are listed at the end of this book.

distinctive in terms of its quality, and we also seek to offer an outlet for work of distinction that might be difficult to place elsewhere.

This brings us to the second feature of the new series, which is the intention to publish mid-length studies, generally within the range of 40,000 to 60,000 words. Such studies are hard to place with existing publishers, for while there are current series that cater for mid-length overviews of particular historiographical topics or themes, there is none of which we are aware that offers similar outlets for original research. *Explorations*, therefore, intends to fill the publishing vacuum between research articles and full-length books (the latter, incidentally, might well be eligible for inclusion in the existing University of Hertfordshire Press series, *Studies in Regional and Local History*).

Third, while we expect this series to become required reading for both academics and students, it is also our intention to ensure that it is of interest and relevance to local historians operating outside an institutional framework. To this end we will ensure that each volume is set at a price that individuals, and not only university libraries, can generally afford. Local and regional history is a subject taught at many levels, from schools to universities. As well as undergraduate modules, there are now numerous M.A. courses in local history, and a high percentage of Ph.D. theses on English social and economic history tackle themes at a local level. Bookshops without a 'local interest' section where history looms large are now rare and history features ever more prominently in other media such as television and radio, testifying to the vitality of research and writing outside the universities, as well as to the sustained growth of popular interest. It is hoped that *Explorations in Local and Regional History* will make a contribution to the continuing efflorescence of our subject.

This preface, finally, serves as a call for proposals. We ask authors to come forward, whether they are studying local themes in relation to particular places (rural or urban), regions, counties or provinces, whether their subject matter comprises social groups (or other groups), landscapes, interactions and movements between places, micro-history or total history. The editors can be consulted informally at the addresses given below, while a formal proposal form is available from the University of Hertfordshire Press at uhpress@herts.ac.uk.

Harold Fox
Centre for English Local History
Marc Fitch Historical Institute
5 Salisbury Road
Leicester LE1 7QR
Fox@leicester.ac.uk

Nigel Goose
Centre for Regional and Local History
Department of Humanities
University of Hertfordshire
College Lane
Hatfield AL10 9AB
N.Goose@herts.ac.uk

Preface

This book is about the history of villages and examines how they worked internally, and how they interacted with the world beyond their boundaries. The question that the book seeks to answer is whether the village was 'self-contained', in the sense of having a self-perpetuating population and a self-sufficient economy. Did the inhabitants have a strong sense of the village's own separate identity, and were they cut off from the outside world? These historical questions recur from one period to another, and it is especially useful to make comparisons over the centuries when detailed documents allow us to probe into the composition of the community and to know something of the mentality of the villagers. If we examine the problem between the thirteenth and the nineteenth centuries, historians of the medieval, early modern and late modern periods can appreciate the direction of long-term changes and learn from the approaches of colleagues facing a similar problem.

This book arose out of a conference held at the University of Leicester in July 2004. The Centre for English Local History acted as host for a gathering which brought together a varied group of historians as speakers. The Centre has no institutional connection with a particular region, but encourages the study of past localities over a long period, the combination of more than one discipline and the use of the comparative method.

The subject evidently awakened widespread interest among local historians, as more than 100 gathered for the conference, and the speakers were encouraged to publish their papers by the response of those who attended.

Many people contributed in various ways to the conference and its publication. Harold Fox and Chris Lewis acted as chairs, Audrey Larrivé, Peter Musgrave and Matt Tompkins helped with its organisation, Andy Isham drew the maps and Pinky Ryan prepared the typescript. With thanks to the Shakespeare Birthplace Trust Record Office, Elizabeth Griffiths, www.heart-of-england.net and Penny Roberts for providing illustrations. The Economic History Society made a generous grant to help to pay for publicity and other costs.

Christopher Dyer

Introduction

CHRISTOPHER DYER

To modern readers the word 'village' has a very positive ring. It is associated in our minds with visually attractive scenes of thatched cottages grouped closely together around a village green, a welcoming inn, a manor house and a stone-walled church. Warm social images are also conveyed by the word, encouraging us to expect 'close-knit' communities in which people depended on each other for labour and goods, practised mutual support, sometimes shared common resources, attended church services and drank and played together. The association of the word 'village' with the mythology of harmonious communities has helped to instil in our minds the concept of the 'self-sufficient village', which could provide for most of its material needs for food, fuel and building material within its own territory. The inhabitants of such places were brought together by religious and political institutions in the form (in different periods) of parish church, manor court, vestry and parish council. In addition to forming a coherent society and orderly self-government, the village, it is often assumed, could be self-sustaining in the composition of its population, as the succession of families from generation to generation would leave limited room for newcomers. In short, rural communities have been conceived as self-contained, able to make their living and conduct their affairs on the basis of their own assets. The inhabitants, it is assumed, identified strongly with their own place of birth and residence. In the more extreme statements of this view, historians have expressed the belief that villages were cut off from their surroundings and were largely unaware of national and international affairs.[1] This view received a severe blow in the 1960s, when Peter Laslett for the early modern period, and Ambrose Raftis for the later Middle Ages, revealed the mobility of the rural population.[2] To some extent we have ever

1. An extreme expression of a prevalent view in the early twentieth century can be found in G. G. Coulton, *The Medieval Village* (Cambridge, 1926), p. 65, in which it is stated that villages were 'self-sufficing', and lived in 'comparative isolation'.
2. P. Laslett, 'Clayworth and Cogenhoe', in P. Laslett, ed., *Family Life and Illicit Love in Earlier Generations* (Cambridge, 1977), pp. 50–101 (first published in 1963); J. A. Raftis, *Tenure and Mobility* (Toronto, 1964).

since been adjusting our interpretations of rural society in the light of the realisation that we are dealing with people prone to migrate, but still retaining some elements of stability, family continuity and attachments to localities.

Another historical generalisation has been the decline of the village, even its death, which has been identified in almost every period of history for which detailed evidence is available. The tendencies that seemed to threaten the village included the stratification of village society on the basis of land and wealth, the disruption of the orderly running of common fields, and ultimately their enclosure, high rates of migration, intrusion of outside authorities into village government, and changes in population even to the point that villages were totally abandoned. The ultimate cause of these threatening developments included the growth of towns, commerce and industry, and demographic changes that could reduce the village's size, or lead to labour shortage, or overload communities with paupers. Lords could have a damaging effect on villages either by neglect or by pressing their own interests too ruthlessly, and state policies also forced villages to adapt to new demands. Religious commitments, which usually unified villages before the Reformation, later became more divisive. The first known claim that villages were faced with a terminal threat was reported to parliament in 1459, and in 2000 in a speech in the House of Commons David Prior MP used the phrase 'self-contained villages' to describe thousands of rural communities that used to have shops, pubs, schools, police houses, churches and chapels (presumably around 1950), and were now suffering from the arrival of cars, intensive farming and the supermarket.[3]

The point to notice, of course, is that through every crisis and threat most villages emerged intact, even though changed. Our concern here is to focus on the idea of the 'self-contained' village. Were villages self-sufficient in their economies? To what extent did village populations persist from generation to generation? Did some periods see more intense migration than others? To what extent did villagers practise endogamy, or did they marry outsiders? Was land inherited through families who were attached to specific holdings? Were villagers aware of life beyond the parish boundary? To what extent were the inhabitants loyal to their community, and did they develop a strong sense of local identity? Did the wider changes in the economy and government erode or strengthen the village's own institutions and society? Did antagonisms between the social strata within the village damage cohesion? Can the history of the village be summed up as a continuous erosion of the original peasant communities, providing for their own needs from the village fields, and living (except for their duties to lord and state) an almost autonomous existence?

3.   M. W. Beresford, *Lost Villages of England* (London, 1954), p. 148; *Hansard* 27 May 2000, column 97. I am indebted to David Brown for this reference.

Before we tackle these questions, a note of caution is needed about the difficulty of generalisation over the whole of a diverse countryside. We also need to remind ourselves about the problems of definition and to consider the meaning of 'village', and the difficulty of distinguishing between nucleated villages and other forms of settlement, and between villages and the manors, parishes and other institutions.

The apparently simple word 'village' carries a range of meanings. Our modern expectation of a village – one could call it an ideal type – in the late medieval period is of a compact group of perhaps twenty to fifty houses, arranged around a church, manor house, mill and water supply. Between 100 and 250 people lived mainly from the produce of open fields, common meadow, pasture and wood, which surrounded the settlement. The inhabitants bound themselves together to pursue common interests, to regulate their fields and to discharge their duties to the state, as the 'community of the vill'. Something resembling this ideal type, at least in terms of size and physical form, can be found in some thousands of examples, mainly in the midlands, and particularly in the period between about 1200 and 1348, when high populations and intense arable agriculture prevailed before the Black Death of 1348–9. Such villages are difficult to investigate for historians, as our records mainly relate to manors, and these institutions, devised to enable lords to extract revenue from the land and its people, did not coincide exactly with a village. Many manors contained only part of the village (the village was often carved up between two, three, or more lords), or a single manor could stretch into two or three villages. A large manor might include within its boundaries a number of settlements.[4] If a village's inhabitants were split between two or more lords' jurisdictions, the manors presented an obstacle to social unity. On the other hand lords also encouraged cooperation among their subordinates, by requiring them to pool animals for ploughing services on the demesne, or by expecting them all to turn out (including women and older children) for a day's harvesting, and by imposing collective financial demands on the customary tenants as a group, such as a payment of tallage levied as a lump sum to which everyone contributed.[5] The state did use the *villata* (often translated as 'vill') as a unit of government, but the vill as a unit of taxation often combined more than one settlement, and indeed the *villa integra* could cover tax payers scattered over a wide area and include a number

4. E. A. Kosminsky, *Studies in the Agrarian History of England in the Thirteenth Century* (Oxford, 1956), pp. 73–5.
5. J. Langdon, *Horses, Oxen and Technological Innovation: The Use of Draught Animals in English Farming from 1066–1500* (Cambridge, 1986), pp. 235–40; P. Vinogradoff, *Villainage in England: Essays in English Mediaeval History* (Oxford, 1892), pp. 174, 283–5; N. Neilson, *Customary Rents* (Oxford, 1910), pp. 90–6.

of villages.[6] The local unit of church government, the parish, often coincided with the territory of the village, and therefore included all of its fields, meadows and pastures. A village might (rarely) be provided with two parish churches, and many parishes included more than one settlement.

In large parts of the country, including much of the south-east and East Anglia, and also in the western regions stretching from Cornwall to the Lake District, nucleated villages of the conventional 'midland' type were relatively scarce, and most people lived in dispersed hamlets and farmsteads.[7] They might be subdivided for administrative purposes into members, tithings, yields, or ends. The inhabitants of the scattered and small settlements tended not to base their economy on open-field agriculture, though they would often cultivate at least part of their arable in subdivided fields, and have some common assets such as woods and pastures, so there was a cooperative dimension in their farming.[8] They might share pastures and woods with neighbouring settlements in a system of intercommoning. They resembled nucleated villages because their lord might require them to participate in collective labour services and rent payment, and they would have a common commitment to the parish church or chapel, so they were used to organising the raising of money. Of course the state grouped them into vills for the purposes of law enforcement, tax collection and public works. In other words, many places functioned institutionally as villages without having the conventional physical or economic attributes.

'Village' therefore refers to a settlement, but not necessarily one that was compactly nucleated; it was usually a unit of agrarian management and cooperative production, but often not on the basis of a fully fledged common-field system. Villages were recognised and used by the state, and they would in many cases coincide with ecclesiastical parishes, but the actual units chosen for these purposes were not always identical with the communities practising common-field farming or sharing common pastures. Contemporaries called these rural units of settlement, agriculture and government 'towns', and that word only acquired its present association with urban societies and economies in relatively recent times.

While we must be aware of these problems of definition, because of the impracticality of studying a village through documentary evidence we are bound to use the records of the manorial lords, the state and the church, which apply to units of administration that overlapped with villages.

6. A. Winchester, 'The medieval vill in the western Lake District: some problems and definitions', *Trans. Cumberland and Westmorland Ant. and Arch. Soc.* 78 (1978), pp. 55–69.
7. B. K. Roberts and S. Wrathmell, *Region and Place: A Study of English Rural Settlement* (London, 2002), pp. 1–31.
8. J. Thirsk, ed., *The English Rural Landscape* (Oxford, 2000), pp. 108–12, 224–7, 269–72.

The institutions and economic units to which villages belonged helped to make them permeable to outside influences. Migration would be especially easy between settlements contained in the same parish or manor; manors in the same estate would be linked across long distances; inter-commoning and marshland reclamation was based on inter-village cooperation.[9]

Turning to later periods some of these problems of definition still apply. The division between regions of nucleation and regions of dispersed settlement survived into the nineteenth and twentieth centuries with some modifications, such as the building of farms in the fields outside nucleated settlements after enclosure, and the growth of industrial villages among scattered rural settlements. The village, as it lost its common fields and pastures, was deprived of its functions as the manager of shared assets. As lords wielded less power, the manor was diminished as an institution, and its court became at best a register of land transfers, though resident squires could still rule effectively over 'close' villages.[10] The parish on the other hand gained in importance, as it was adopted by the state as the unit of local government and more specifically to administer the poor law. The secular administration of the parish took over many of the old functions of the vill, and became separated from the religious functions of the local church.

The changes in institutions will be apparent as the essays that form this book trace changes in village society over more than five centuries.

9. H. S. A. Fox, 'Co-operation between rural communities in medieval England', in P. Sereno and M. L. Sturani, eds, *Rural Landscape between State and Local: Communities in Europe Past and Present* (Alessandrie, 1998), pp. 31–48.

10. On the decline of the manor court: P. D. A. Harvey, *Manorial Records* (British Records Association, rev. edn, 1999), pp. 55–68. For close villages: B. Short, 'The evolution of contrasting communities within rural England', in B. Short, ed., *The English Rural Community. Image and Analysis* (Cambridge, 1992), pp. 19–43.

1

Were late medieval English villages 'self-contained'?

CHRISTOPHER DYER

The real test for the idea that villages were in the past 'self-contained' lies in the medieval period, as historians commonly assume that it was always in some early pre-modern arcadia that self-sustaining and self-regulating peasant communities flourished. A really remote period would be the tenth and eleventh centuries, when nucleated villages and the well-defined territories of perhaps 2 or 3 square miles attached to them were relatively young. But the written evidence from that period cannot allow us to probe into village society, so we must begin our inquiry with the period when documents for the first time become abundant, after 1250.

The aim of this essay is to survey English rural society in the period between the thirteenth and the sixteenth centuries, with the purpose of defining the extent to which villages can be regarded as 'self-contained'. The themes of landholding, migration, economy and culture will be addressed. My examples will often be drawn from the west midlands, though I will attempt to reflect regional differences, across the country and also within the west midlands.

Landholding

Part of the concept of the 'self-contained village' is that its houses were occupied by families who, by inheriting land from generation to generation, ensured a continuity of population over long periods of time. This was more than just a matter of individual families' sense of connection to particular holdings, as the households of neighbours became used to interacting with one another in village networks of lenders and borrowers, marriage partners and co-workers. The well-established families would tend to occupy offices in the village, and they would ensure that traditions and memories were carried forward through time.

Peasant inheritance was not a myth, but featured prominently in some regions and in specific periods. When the inheritance patterns in a series of manorial court rolls in the midlands and south are investigated, a high proportion of transfers of customary holdings in the period 1270–1348 consisted of the acquisition of land by heirs after the death of their parents, together with the surrenders of land by tenants to members of their own family. A specialised example of the latter type, transfers between living family members, arose from retirement arrangements, when elderly or incapacitated tenants handed over the holding to their heirs, in exchange for a promise that they would be maintained for the rest of their lives.[1] Another characteristic grant of property was made by a father to a younger son or a daughter, that is members of the next generation who under the rules of primogeniture had no expectation of inheriting the main family holding, but could be given parcels of land acquired by the father by purchase or by clearance from the waste.[2]

At Halesowen in Worcestershire (a manor that contained a number of settlements), in the late thirteenth and early fourteenth centuries a high figure, 63 per cent, of the transfers of landholdings within the family can be calculated by putting together both inheritance after death and transactions between living parties. The percentage of land (as distinct from holdings) that passed between family members was even greater, 80 per cent,[3] because the larger units of tenure, the yardland and half-yardland (c. 30 and 15 acres respectively) were mostly inherited. Small parcels of land, such as acres of cleared land (assarts) were more often transferred between families.

The figures are not quite as high on the manors of the bishops of Winchester, which stretched across southern England from Surrey to Somerset. From a total of 35,000 land transactions between 1269 and 1349 which have been analysed, transfers within the family amounted to 46 per cent of the total, and again inheritance and grants in life to family members were higher if the calculation is confined to the yardlands or fractions of yardlands.[4] At Witney in Oxfordshire, one of the manors of the estate sited within a royal forest, and surrounded by woodland, less than 20 per cent of holdings were inherited. When the many assarts and parcels of land, however, are taken out of the calculation, 46 per cent of transfers took place within the family, three-quarters of these by inheritance. This emphasis on movements of land within the family on the Winchester manors as a whole tended to increase in the early fourteenth century, as in the decades

1.   R. M. Smith, 'The English peasantry, 1250–1650', in T. Scott, ed., *The Peasantries of Europe* (London, 1998), pp. 359–60; Z. Razi, 'The myth of the immutable English family', *Past and Present* 140 (1993), pp. 3–44; R. M. Smith, 'The manorial court and the elderly tenant in late medieval England', in M. Pelling and R. M. Smith, eds, *Life, Death and the Elderly* (London, 1991), pp. 39–61.
2.   Z. Razi, 'Family, land and the village community in late medieval England', in T. H. Aston, ed., *Landlords, Peasants and Politics in Medieval England* (Cambridge, 1987), pp. 366–7.
3.   Ibid., p. 361.
4.   M. Page, 'The peasant land market on the estate of the bishopric of Winchester before the Black Death', in R. Britnell, ed., *The Winchester Pipe Rolls and Medieval English Society* (Woodbridge, 2003), pp. 62–4.

before 1300 the proportion hovered around 40 per cent, but rose to 48–9 per cent in 1300–20. The importance of inheritance and the continuity of families varied from manor to manor, depending on local landscapes and societies: on such chalkland manors as East Meon and Hambledon, with their many standard holdings measured in yardlands and tendency to live on a regime of sheep and corn husbandry, movements of land between relatives were twice as frequent as at Witney with its wooded landscape, more pastoral economy and numerous smallholders. At the centre of Witney manor lay a market town, which stimulated the buying and selling of parcels of land.[5]

The story of the tenure of a yardland at Bishop's Waltham in Hampshire, another manor on the Winchester estate, beginning in the 1220s, illustrates the tenacity of a family's connection with a particular holding, and also warns us of the traps awaiting those who seek to trace family succession in a period of unstable surnames. The land was acquired in 1227 by Philip of Hoo, passed to his son German (or Jermayn) of Hoo in 1269, and it in turn went to his son (Philip's grandson), William Jermayn, at some time after 1286. In 1328 the holding was surrendered by William (by then elderly) to his daughter Isabella, who was married to Andrew of Bodenham. By 1338 Andrew had died, but Isabella remained as the tenant, and after marriage to John le Spencier (also known as Parker) she passed the land on to Alice her daughter in 1361. At various stages the land came temporarily into the hands of guardians and other non-relatives such as Spencier, and was held by tenants with four different surnames, but essentially remained in the blood line for five generations over 134 years.[6] The high quality of the Winchester estate documents allow us to reconstruct the descent of this piece of land, but there would be obvious dangers of assuming a lack of hereditary succession if we depended on surnames alone as evidence of family links. This example is rather extreme as it goes back into the period before 1270, for which documents only rarely survive, and when surnames were still fluid. Names gained in stability by the fourteenth century, but this would not help us to detect inheritance through the female line, which would lead to a male tenant from a different family taking over the holding.[7]

A contrast is provided by rural East Anglia, where the standard tenements had broken down by the thirteenth century, and commerce had a strong influence. The records of courts are filled with a seemingly endless list of tenants coming to the court to surrender an acre, half-acre, or rood (quarter-acre) of land to an

5.   Ibid., pp. 63, 73–4, 79–80.
6.   J. Z. Titow, *English Rural Society 1200–1350* (London, 1969), pp. 186–8.
7.   Z. Razi, 'The erosion of the family land bond in the late fourteenth and fifteenth centuries: a methodological note', in R. M. Smith, ed., *Land, Kinship and Lifecycle* (Cambridge, 1984), pp. 295–304.

apparently unrelated tenant, and although the documents noted only the payment of an entry fine to the lord (which was often set at quite a high level of at least 2s. od. per acre), the incoming tenant was also paying money to the person who surrendered the land. In other words, a lively, even a heated, land market had developed, and this meant that in the decades before the Black Death the percentage of transfers between family members could be as low as 19 per cent (at Redgrave, Suffolk).[8]

After 1349, inheritance declined, and continuity in village families diminished. At Halesowen, thanks to Razi's meticulous reconstitution of families and kin connections, in the period 1349–1430 holdings continued to descend to relatives, but often, in the absence of a son, the heirs were nephews or cousins of the previous tenant, who had surnames different from their predecessor. These more remote relatives often came to claim their holding from settlements outside Halesowen.[9]

From 1430 onwards at Halesowen, as elsewhere, even if more distant kin relationships are known, most land was being transferred between parties who were unrelated.[10] In the period after 1430 a manor can be found, such as Thornbury in Gloucestershire, where as many as a half of holdings passed from one family member to another.[11] But in many west-midland manors the proportion of transfers between relatives fell to 10 or 20 per cent of the total, and one can find manors in which, although they have ample documentation, in some ten-year periods no land at all was inherited or granted to a family member. Bishop's Hampton in Warwickshire, later called Hampton Lucy, had originally included two villages, but one, Hatton-on-Avon, was abandoned in the late fourteenth century. Hampton itself shows various signs of a profound malaise in the mid- and late fifteenth century, when few or no heirs wished to take over their families' holding.[12]

As a result of the discontinuities in families' tenure of land in the fifteenth century, many entries in rentals sought to identify each holding so that it could be located in earlier documents. The clerk writing the rental gave the names of one or more earlier tenants, and states the name attached to the holding, usually of some long-departed tenant family. Often the holding's name, the former tenants' and

8. R. Smith, 'Families and their land in an area of partible inheritance: Redgrave, Suffolk 1260–1320', in Smith, ed., Land, Kinship and Lifecycle, pp. 182–4.
9. Razi, 'Family, land and community', pp. 379–81.
10. Razi, 'Immutable English family', pp. 28–36.
11. C. Dyer, 'Changes in the link between families and land in the west midlands in the fourteenth and fifteenth centuries', in Smith., ed., Land, Kinship and Lifecycle, pp. 306–7.
12. C. Dyer, Lords and Peasants in a Changing Society: The Estates of the Bishopric of Worcester, 680–1540 (Cambridge, 1980), pp. 302–3, 359–60.

the present tenant's names are all different. So for example at Bishop's Cleeve in Gloucestershire in a rental of 1475 a holding is described thus: 'John Sewell holds one messuage and 6 acres of customary land called Gamons, formerly held by William Fowler', and another entry states that 'Thomas Yardyngton holds one messuage and 6 acres formerly held by Thomas Wever and before that by John Smythe'.[13]

Such evidence should not be taken at face value, in view of the gender bias which meant that holdings inherited by a married daughter would appear under her husband's name in the rental and court rolls. Most sets of records do not allow us to identify nephews and in-laws, so the degree to which inheritance declined in the fifteenth century remains uncertain. There must, however, have been a declining trend in succession within the family. If we can observe a drop in inheritance in the male line from about 50 per cent to about 10 per cent, that is in itself a significant change, and inheritance through females is likely to have also declined. A confirmation comes from the number of occasions in the fifteenth century that a holding remained 'in the lord's hands' after a tenant died or surrendered it. Had a relative been waiting to take over the land, it would not have been left unoccupied for a few months or even years.

These technical details provide a route to understanding the attitudes of peasants towards the land and the villages in which their houses and lands lay. If Razi is right to argue that midland peasants had in c. 1300 a sense of lineage, pride in past inheritance, and a feeling that they were acting as trustees for a family holding which would pass to future generations, this would help to tie people to a particular village. Some would dispute this depiction of peasant mentality, or at least regard it as confined to a particular region and period, but everyone can agree that by the mid-fifteenth century the land–family bond had been weakened. Peasants were prepared to acquire and shed holdings for convenience or profit. They built up accumulations of land which had previously been held by different families, and then disposed of them to another range of families when they had no need of them. Land was quite plentiful, and could sometimes be acquired cheaply, which reduced the desire of tenants to hang onto land and keep it for their heirs. The number of heirs declined with the reduction in the size of families, and those who survived into adulthood could acquire land for themselves, without waiting for their fathers' holdings. The pragmatism of peasants is well indicated by the renewal of an interest in inheritance in the sixteenth century, as land values increased and holdings became relatively scarce.[14]

13. Worcestershire Record Office (hereafter WRO), BA 2636, ref. 009:1, 161/92113 3/6.
14. J. Whittle, *The Development of Agrarian Capitalism. Land and Labour in Norfolk 1440–1580* (Oxford, 2000), pp. 102–10.

To conclude, the evidence of landholding, inheritance and the land market strengthens the chances of encountering a self-contained village in the thirteenth century outside East Anglia. In the late fourteenth century and especially in the fifteenth in all regions the transfer of land reduced the continuities of family succession and encouraged migration, making the more extreme modern conceptions of the self-perpetuating peasant community impossible to imagine.

Migration

The tendency of medieval countrymen and women to uproot themselves is attested from our earliest abundant records in the thirteenth century. They flowed into towns in considerable numbers, as urban dwellers doubled as a proportion of the whole population between 1086 and c. 1300. A backwash of migrants from the towns into the villages left a scatter of surnames such as 'de London' and 'de Aylesbury' in tax records in Hertfordshire villages in 1307.[15] The movement of people into areas of land clearance and fenland drainage can be detected not just in the surnames, but also in the long-term rise in population density. These were merely the more easily visible, long-distance and coordinated migrations, which need to be understood alongside the constant small-scale and short-distance journeys from village to village.

Movements of people in the period 1250–1348 can be traced in a number of ways. The number of males over twelve years old who were sworn into tithings in Essex villages in the early fourteenth century allows the calculation that each year about 4 per cent of them left each village, and 5 per cent entered, which if sustained over many years would lead to a considerable turnover in the villages' inhabitants.[16] Serfs were not supposed to leave the manor without the permission of their lord, and many manors demanded a payment, chevage or head money, for the licence to live away. Before 1348 many serfs' sons and daughters moved, and the lord could be quite relaxed about a breach of the rules that did him no great harm, as the demand for land ensured that every tenancy would normally be filled, and as labour was plentiful manorial officials had no difficulty in recruiting farm servants to operate the ploughs, carts, sheepfolds and dairies of the demesne. These emigrants were therefore only mentioned occasionally in the court records, though one lord, Spalding Priory, compiled lists of serfs in the late thirteenth century; in one of these we are told that thirty-two of them had left two villages.[17]

15. J. Brooker and S. Flood, eds, *Hertfordshire Lay Subsidy Rolls, 1307 and 1334* (Herts. Record Pubs, 14, 1998), pp. 102, 120, 125.
16. L. Poos, 'The rural population of Essex in the later middle ages', *Econ. Hist. Rev.*, 2nd ser., 37 (1985), pp. 515–30.
17. E. D. Jones, 'Some Spalding priory vagabonds of the 1260s', *Hist. Research* 73 (2000), pp. 93–104.

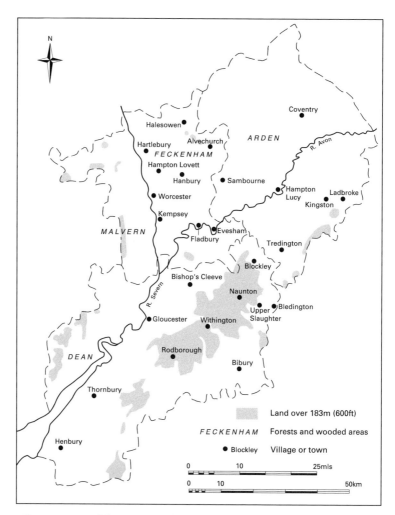

Figure 1.1 Map of the counties of Gloucestershire, Warwickshire and Worcestershire, showing places mentioned in text

The manorial authorities were also concerned about villagers who harboured immigrants: these strangers had not been sworn into tithing, and therefore posed a threat to order. They were presumably being brought in as employees of the peasants, and often as living-in servants. On the manors of Glastonbury Abbey servants (*garciones*), often employed by the tenants, were listed when they made a small payment to the lord, and they were sometimes said to have left for another place. On this and other estates there are references to 'strangers' and 'incomers' who owed a payment to the lord.[18]

18. J. A Raftis, *Tenure and Mobility* (Toronto, 1964), pp. 130–5; H. S. A. Fox, 'Exploitation of the landless by lords and tenants in early medieval England', in Z. Razi and R. M. Smith, eds, *Medieval Society and the Manor Court* (Oxford, 1996), pp. 518–39.

After 1348 migration became much more controversial, and was therefore more carefully recorded. The movement of serfs away from the manor threatened to leave holdings untenanted, and a shortage of labour made it difficult for lords to recruit enough ploughmen, harvesters and other workers. The future of serfdom itself was endangered, as in their new homes the migrants could shed their servile status, and the hereditary condition of neifty by blood (those personally tainted with servile status were called *nativi de sanguine*) would die out. Consequently manorial court rolls from the latter decades of the fourteenth century through to the early sixteenth can contain lists of *nativi* who had left, with the places to which they had gone, followed by an order that the relatives of the offender should ensure that they return, under a stiff financial penalty, such as 3s. 4d. or 6s. 8d. These orders were usually ignored; the absenteeism persisted, and in the long run the *nativi* disappeared from the memory of the manorial officials. The withering of serfdom shows that late medieval mobility affected not just the well-being of individuals – it changed institutions.[19]

A typical list is found in a court roll of a manor (coincident with a village) belonging to Evesham Abbey at Sambourne in Warwickshire in 1472.[20] Twenty names are mentioned, in the first entry in the business of the court, and were stated to have been 'presented by the homage', so the information came from local people, the former neighbours of the people who had left. As is usually the case, the destinations of the emigrants mostly lay between 7 and 20 miles: only five had gone further afield. The most adventurous journeys are worth a mention: Robert Clopton was living in Rockingham Forest in Northamptonshire, and two of his sons, Richard and John, together with his brother Thomas were said to be in Kent (one notes that the location became vaguer at longer distances, as if detailed knowledge of individual villages faded at a distance of about 20 miles). Nine were living in towns (Evesham, Coventry and Daventry), which is a rather higher proportion than is normal: often towns account for about a third of the migrants' place of residence. In some records, such as those of Hampton Lovett (Worcestershire) we can follow the movements of individuals who did not remain at their original destination, and then they can be observed passing from country to town and back again.[21] The Sambourne list gives us some clues as to the role of the migrants in their new place of residence. William, son of Robert Wylcockis, was said to have been at the rectory of the church of Naunton in the Cotswolds, presumably working as a servant, and Agnes, daughter of John Robyns had married Thomas Suard of Evesham. Both William and Agnes were young, judging

19. R. H. Hilton, *The Decline of Serfdom in Medieval England* (London, 1969), pp. 32–5.
20. Shakespeare Birthplace Trust Records Office, Stratford-upon-Avon (hereafter SBT), DR 5/2357.
21. R. K. Field, 'Migration in the later middle ages: the case of the Hampton Lovett villeins', *Mid. Hist.* 8 (1983), pp. 36, 42.

Table 1.1 Tenant surnames at Kingston, Warwickshire, 1386–1430

1386–7	1393–4	1426	1430
Aubyn	Aubyn		
Barker			
Cammville	Cammville	Cammville	
Caudron			
Clerebord			
Commander	Commander		Commander
Derlove	Derlove	Derlove	Derlove
Knyght	Knyght		
Mason	Mason		
Parker			
Peyto	Peyto	Peyto	Peyto
Sheperde	Sheperde		
Symple	Symple		
Whelewryght	Whelewryght		
Werlone			
	Neucome	Neucome	
	Tasker		
		Assho	
		Blyke	Blyke
		Bolle	Bolle
		Boteller	Boteller
		Clerk	Clerk
		Coly	Coly
		Draper	Draper
		Lovecok	Lovecok
		Philippes	
		Smith	Smith
			Perkyns

Sources: British Library, Egerton rolls 2106, 2108; SBT, DR98/438, /463a.

from their identification by their father's name. Some young emigrants were said to have become apprentices in their new place of residence. An analysis of 346 serfs who left nineteen manors of Worcester Cathedral Priory in the period 1349–89 shows that females made up a third of them, and many of them were young. If the unmarried males are included, the youthful element accounts for near to a half of the total. Many of these young people were probably moving from their native village to be employed as servants.[22]

Serfs were a special case, as they had very good reasons to move. Information based on a wider section of society, however, confirms the picture of mobility; for example from those giving evidence to church courts in late fifteenth-century Essex, 76 per cent had not lived in the same place throughout their lives.[23]

The most abundant information relates to tenants, both customary and free,

22. P. Hargreaves, 'Change in relationships between lord and tenants on manors of Worcester Cathedral Priory 1340–1390' (unpublished Ph.D. thesis, Birmingham, 1997), pp. 243–70.
23. L. Poos, *A Rural Society after the Black Death: Essex 1350–1525* (Cambridge, 1991), pp. 166–79.

who are listed in rentals and found in court rolls taking or surrendering holdings. The tenants of Kingston, sometimes called Little Chesterton, in the parish of Chesterton in Warwickshire were listed four times between 1387 and 1430. The manor coincided with the village. As Table 1.1 shows, of the fifteen family names of tenants that were listed in 1387, fourteen were likely to have been resident, as the Peytos were lords of the manor of Chesterton. Five had departed by 1394, seven more went between 1394 and 1426, and four between 1426 and 1430, leaving only two long staying families, the Derloves and the Commanders, but the latter were recorded as living in Chesterton, so there was only one family that remained in Kingston during the whole of the forty-three years in which we can observe the householders of this village.[24]

Kingston had lost a number of tenants before 1387, as there were probably at least twenty-six separately tenanted holdings before the Black Death of 1348–9, which were concentrated into the hands of fifteen people by 1387. There had already been a major change in the village families, as not a single name recorded in the tax list of 1332 reappears in 1387.[25] New tenants had come in after 1387, but not enough to compensate for the losses, and only eleven tenants were left in 1430. The newcomers did not always stay for long, or at least they were not succeeded by heirs in the male line, as four of the new names recorded in 1394 and 1426 did not appear in 1430. Kingston's decline accelerated, and within fifty years was totally deserted. In this period of Kingston's demise, when its population was very unstable and dwindling, the rate of movement of family names can be calculated as 2.2 per cent per annum.

Comparison with larger and less depressed places shows that the rate of emigration was lower, but was still high enough to ensure that a large majority of families died out in the male line in a period of fifty years. Ladbroke, not far from Kingston, lay in the Feldon district of Warwickshire and was therefore another nucleated village practising open-field husbandry. The rentals of 1374, 1389, 1446 and 1457 show that from an original thirty-one families in 1374, only four remained after eighty-one years.[26] This amounts to a loss of *c.* 1 per cent per annum, but the pace quickened between 1389 and 1446 to 1.3 per cent. A similar figure, in the region of an annual turnover of 1 per cent, is also found on the manor of Kempsey where the tenants lived in ten nucleated hamlets, which followed a mixed-farming regime in irregular fields just outside the champion landscape of south Worcestershire. Of 103 names appearing in the court rolls in

24. British Library, Egerton rolls 2106, 2108; SBT, DR98/438, /463a.
25. W. F. Carter, ed., *Lay Subsidy Roll for Warwickshire of 6 Edward III (1332)* (Dugdale Soc., 6, 1926), p. 22.
26. TNA:PRO, SC12 16/27; 16/28; 16/29; 16/30.

Table 1.2 Worcestershire villages: persistence of surnames recorded in the lay subsidies of 1327 and 1524–5

	Champion villages (10)[1]	Woodland villages (9)[2]
No. of surnames in 1327	208	302
No. of these surnames still there in 1524–5	16	25
Percentage still there	8	8

Notes:
1. Alderminster, Badsey, Bishampton, Bricklehampton, Eckington, Elmley Castle, Flyford Flavel, Great Comberton, Sedgeberrow, Wickhamford
2. Eldersfield, Elmley Lovett, Feckenham, Frankley, Hanley Castle, Martley, Mathon, Stoke Prior, Yardley
Sources: F. J. Eld, ed., *Lay Subsidy Roll for the County of Worcester, 1 Edward III* (Worcs. Hist. Soc., 1895); M. Faraday, ed., *Worcestershire Taxes of the 1520s* (Worcs. Hist. Soc., 19, 2003).

1432–41, twenty-five were still there in the period 1499–1507.[27] In other parts of midland England, such as the Huntingdonshire manors of Holywell cum Needingworth and Warboys, the rate of disappearance of families between 1350 and 1449 was on a similar scale, with a definitely quickening pace after 1400.[28] More stability is apparent at Kibworth Harcourt in Leicestershire where 27 per cent of the surnames recorded in 1412 survived in 1527, making a turnover of 0.63 per cent annually.[29] Here a longer perspective could be taken, and of thirty-nine surnames in 1280, seven survived in 1527. The majority of family names changed, but the proportion of those that remained (18 per cent) cannot be regarded as negligible.

Rather than depending on examples, in search of some comparative understanding of patterns of migration in and out of villages in different environments, a sample of villages in Worcestershire has been analysed in Table 1.2. This is based on the lists of taxpayers for the 1327 lay subsidy, and the subsidies of 1524–5.[30] The county was quite sharply divided: nucleated villages and champion landscapes predominated in the south and east, in the vale of Evesham, and the clay lowlands to the north-west of the Avon valley. In the north and west of the county the woodlands included the Forest of Feckenham and Malvern Chase, with their dispersed settlements, irregular field systems and 'old enclosures'. Nineteen villages were selected with legible entries in both taxes, which were unequivocally located in either the champion or the woodland

27. Dyer, *Lords and Peasants*, p. 366.
28. Razi, 'Immutable English family', p. 35
29. C. Howell, 'Peasant inheritance customs in the midlands, 1280–1700', in J. Goody, J. Thirsk and E. P. Thompson, eds, *Family and Inheritance: Rural Society in Western Europe 1200–1800* (Cambridge, 1976), pp. 123–7; eadem, *Land, Family and Inheritance in Transition. Kibworth Harcourt 1280–1700* (Cambridge, 1983), p. 241.
30. F. J. Eld, ed., *Lay Subsidy Roll for the County of Worcester, 1 Edward III* (Worcs. Hist. Soc., 1895); M. Faraday, ed., *Worcestershire Taxes of the 1520s* (Worcs. Hist. Soc., 19, 2003).

Table 1.3 Gloucestershire villages: persistence of surnames, 1327–81, and 1381–1522/5

Village	Bledington	Upper Slaughter	Rodborough
No. of surnames in 1327	17	8	16
No. of these still there in 1381	8	2	4
Percentage still there	47	25	25
No. of surnames in 1381	30	18	30
No. of these still there in 1522/5	2	1	2
Percentage still there	7	6	7
No. of surnames in 1327	17	8	16
No. of these still there in 1522/5	0	1	0
Percentage still there	0	13	0

Sources: P. Franklin, *The Taxpayers of Medieval Gloucestershire* (Stroud, 1993); C. C. Fenwick, ed., *The Poll Taxes of 1377, 1379 and 1381* (British Academy Records of Social and Economic History, new ser., 27, 1998); R. Hoyle, *The Military Survey of Gloucestershire, 1522* (Bristol and Glos. Arch. Soc., Glos. Record Ser., 6, 1993); TNA: PRO, E179/113/189; 113/213.

landscapes, with a bias in favour of larger villages to give a substantial sample. Settlements that shrank severely in the two centuries and those on the outskirts of towns were also excluded. As can be seen, an overall 8 per cent of 1327 surnames persisted in both types of landscape until 1524–5. Continuity of names varied from village to village, from none to 15 per cent. The degree of survival may be exaggerated, as common names such as Smith and Tailor probably reappeared rather than surviving continuously. On the other hand, differences in the spelling of names, or even changes of name, may have concealed continuity in some families.

The main disadvantage in using tax records is that they exclude the poorer section of society. In the case of the 1327 lay subsidy a plausible estimate would be that 60 per cent of the rural population were exempted, and as the poor might be expected to be especially mobile, the percentage of surnames surviving from the whole community is likely to have been lower than 8 per cent. Tax records with lists of names also appear at widely separated periods, as the names of individual subsidy payers were not recorded by central government between 1332 and 1524. It is worth looking at the poll tax records of 1377–81, as they contain lists of tax payers' names. Gloucestershire has a 1327 subsidy, patchy poll-tax returns, a military survey of 1522, and incomplete records of the 1524–5 subsidies.[31] The persistence of surnames in three villages in different landscapes is analysed in Table 1.3, which shows that in the clay lowlands of the Evenlode valley (at

31. P. Franklin, *The Taxpayers of Medieval Gloucestershire* (Stroud, 1993); C. C. Fenwick, ed., *The Poll Taxes of 1377, 1379 and 1381* (British Academy Records of Social and Economic History, new ser., 27, 1998) ; R. Hoyle, *The Military Survey of Gloucestershire*, 1522 (Bristol and Glos. Arch. Soc., Glos. Record Ser., 6, 1993); TNA: PRO, E179/113/189; 113/213.

Table 1.4 Bishopric of Worcester manors, continuity in tenant surnames, 1299–1544

Cotswold manors	Bibury	Blockley	Withington
No. of surnames, 1299	27	89	48
No. of these still there in 1544	0	0	1
Percentage still there	0	0	2

Champion manors (Avon and Stour valleys) Fladbury		Hampton	Tredington
No. of surnames, 1299	56	47	54
No. of those still there in 1544	3	1	0
Percentage still there	5	2	0

Woodland manors	Alvechurch	Hanbury	
No. of surnames, 1299	85	65	
No. of those still there in 1544	3	3	
Percentage still there	4	5	

Severn Valley manors	Hartlebury	Henbury	
No. of surnames, 1299	80	94	
No. of those still there in 1544	7	7	
Percentage still there	9	7	

Sources: M. Hollings, ed., *The Red Book of Worcester* (Worcs. Hist. Soc., 1934–50); WRO, BA 2636, ref. 009:1, 18/47765.

Bledington), in the Cotswold village of Upper Slaughter, and in the wooded industrialising settlement of Rodborough a sizeable minority of families were still resident half a century after 1327, but most of them died out or moved in the succeeding 140 years. The comparison has not been pursued here on a larger scale because of the dangers of building too much on records which are very different, as the poll tax in theory included all families, while the subsidies were much more selective.

Finally a comparison can be made between lists of tenants on ten manors of the bishops of Worcester made in 1299 and 1544 (Table 1.4).[32] These are not villages but large manors, most of which included a number of settlements. Tredington manor, for example, contained three small villages, and Alvechurch and Hanbury dozens of hamlets and scattered farms. The value of the records is their inclusion of tenants of all kinds, including smallholders and cottagers who would not have contributed to royal taxation. Their long-term possession by an ecclesiastical institution means that no allowance needs to be made for variations in lordship, which may have influenced the different patterns of migration between taxation vills used in compiling Tables 1.2 and 1.3. In this sample the differences are clear, with virtually no continuity of families in the Cotswolds, a

32. M. Hollings, ed., *The Red Book of Worcester* (Worcs. Hist. Soc., 1934–50); WRO, BA 2636, ref. 009:1, 18/47765.

characteristic suggested by other manorial studies, such as those of the estates of Winchcombe Abbey.[33] Only a very modest number of families survived in the champion manors of the Avon and Stour valleys, but the minority that survived in the woodlands or the Severn valley, especially the latter, was not insignificant.

Manorial records allow us to suggest the factors that encouraged migration in one place and inhibited it in another. On the Cotswold and champion manors the demand for land declined especially sharply in the late fourteenth and fifteenth centuries, which is reflected in the reduction in the annual rents paid for standard holdings. At Bibury in the Cotswolds, for example, the payment per annum for a yardland of about 48 acres declined from 19s. in 1299 to 8s. in the fifteenth century, while at Henbury at the mouth of the Severn rent remained quite high: a yardland paid 25s. in the fifteenth century compared with 28s. before the Black Death of 1348–9.[34] The entry fines paid by an incoming tenant, the most sensitive indicator of the intensity of the land market, in the early years of the sixteenth century reached a high mean of £8 per yardland at Henbury, between a pound or two at Hanbury in the woodlands of north Worcestershire, and were well below a pound at Bibury and Hampton (a champion manor in the Avon valley). Transfers within the family were more commonly encountered in the woodland and Severn valley manors than in the champion and Cotswold ones.[35] These differences were related to the economic opportunities experienced in these different localities. Champion and Cotswold field systems were designed to grow corn in great quantity, and although the peasants adapted to the reduced demand for cereals, they were at a disadvantage compared with their counterparts in settlements with mixed land use and enclosed fields, who enjoyed a greater degree of flexibility in developing the pastoral side of their agriculture. In the Severn valley in particular the villagers had better access to urban markets, and Henbury lay on the edge of the large town of Bristol.

These findings can be supported from studies of migratory trends in other parts of England. The Berkshire manor of Coleshill, in a champion district not far from the southern edge of the Bishop of Worcester's estate, experienced an extreme degree of instability by the end of the fourteenth century, and even the apparently prosperous yeoman families who built up large holdings in the fifteenth century did not remain for long.[36] In contrast the woodland communities of Havering atte Bower in Essex, lying on a main road leading into London,

33. D. Aldred and C. Dyer, 'A medieval Cotswold village: Roel, Gloucestershire', *Trans. Bristol and Glos. Arch. Soc.* 109 (1991), pp. 139–70.
34. Dyer, *Lords and Peasants*, p. 284.
35. Ibid., pp. 287–92.
36. R. Faith, 'Berkshire: fourteenth and fifteenth centuries', in P. D. A. Harvey, ed., *The Peasant Land Market in Medieval England* (Oxford, 1984), pp. 154–8.

included in their population in 1497 'a core of seventy-seven families who had been resident for three generations'.[37]

Who stayed and who moved? On the bishopric of Worcester estates the long stayers included some better-off and privileged inhabitants, including a few gentry or near gentry families, such as the Throckmortons at Fladbury and the Hanburys of Hanbury. The Elvyns at the latter place were among the tenants of more substantial customary holdings, who later acquired some free land, and the three surviving families at Alvechurch were all freeholders. Among the long-staying families at Henbury were the Mattoks who had held a customary yardland in the late thirteenth century, and the Romes whose smaller customary holding had been supplemented by land held on lease. At Hartlebury the Stowres and Wylmotts were both yardlanders (see pp. 32–9 for similar findings in later centuries).

Those who emigrated included the cottagers and smallholders who hoped to better themselves by acquiring more land and well-rewarded employment. Customary tenants who were categorised as personally unfree (*nativi de sanguine*) had, as we have seen, a particular motive to move to another manor where their freedom would be assumed. All kinds of tenant would contract marriage outside their villages, and the suspicion must be that most peasants found their partners in villages other than their own.[38] Poverty forced some emigration, for example, to towns where charity was concentrated. The demoralised poor might drift into the 'sink villages', where criminals and other antisocial elements congregated. Those of which we are best informed were decayed villages in the champion, such as Bishop's Hampton (now Hampton Lucy) which has already been identified as a village where only rarely did a son inherit his father's holding. In the 1450s and 1460s the manor court at Hampton heard complaints of brothel keeping, suspicious strangers, and 'badly governed' inhabitants.[39] Hopes of 'betterment' might take emigrants to prospering rural settlements, such as those with access to town markets, or those offering industrial employment.

A flow of immigrants would in many villages balance those who were leaving. Newcomers came into the manor court to become tenants of vacant holdings, or in some prearranged transfer took the land surrendered by an outgoing tenant. A tendency in the fifteenth century that was no doubt welcomed by lords, but posed a threat to the health of the village, lay in the acquisition of land by outsiders as an investment. Clothiers took land in Essex textile making villages, or in Bedfordshire townsmen acquired rural property, and gentry tenants took on holdings of customary land which they would have thought beneath their dignity

---

37. M. K. McIntosh, *Autonomy and Community. The Royal Manor of Havering, 1200–1500* (Cambridge, 1986), p. 222.
38. Dyer, *Lords and Peasants*, p. 367.
39. WRO, BA 2636, ref. 009:1, 164/92183, 92186, 92187, 92188.

Figure 1.2 Hampton Lucy (Bishop's Hampton), Warwickshire, a sink village in the fifteenth
century. These cottages were probably built in the seventeenth century, shown in a photograph
of *c.* 1900 (Shakespeare Birthplace Trust Record Office)

in earlier times.[40] At the opposite end of the social hierarchy were the subtenants
who would cultivate the land of absentees, but might also acquire temporarily part
or all of the holding of some resident villagers, which means that the lists
compiled by lords of those responsible for rent payment or liable to attend the
manor court would not record those who actually worked the land.

Contemporaries sometimes complained about the illicit immigrants, vagrants
and undesirables who came into the village, though authorities in towns seem to
have been more exercised by this problem. Welsh people, who must constantly
have moved through the west-midland counties, are rarely mentioned in manorial
records, one exception being at Hartlebury in Worcestershire in 1473 when a
villager broke the rules by allowing Welsh drovers to occupy the common pasture
with their beasts.[41]

40. P. Schofield, 'Extranei and the market for customary land on a Westminster Abbey manor in the
    fifteenth century', *Ag. Hist. Rev.* 49 (2001), 9–16; A. Jones, 'Bedfordshire: fifteenth century', in
    Harvey, ed., *Land Market*, pp. 231–5.
41. WRO, BA 2636, ref. 009:1, 169/92372.

Migration might be regarded both by contemporaries and historians as damaging to the social cohesion of villages, but this would not always have been the case. Communities could absorb newcomers, judging from the speed with which they were brought into the various offices of village government. An example from north Worcestershire is George Underhill senior, who left Hampton Lovett in about 1479, and settled in Hartlebury, 5 miles away.[42] He acquired a landholding of middling size – three nooks that contained about 15 acres – and embarked on a twenty-year career as a brewer and seller of ale, and a dealer in bread, candles and meat. In 1482 he acted as churchwarden, and five years later he was serving as a juror in the manor court. Such a rapid absorption into the governing elite would be a necessity in a decaying village like Kingston in Chesterton (see above p. 15) where the turnover of tenants was so extreme, but Hartlebury was not in such a plight.

It may well have been healthy for a community to replenish its population, and bring into its upper ranks those who had useful outside experience. They might spread knowledge of new agricultural methods or, as in Underhill's case, introduce retailing skills. The period when migration was most rapid, the fifteenth century, coincided with innovations in community life, when churchwardens developed new methods for money-raising, especially for church building, and fraternities in eastern England became more numerous and active.[43] Villages subject to much to-ing and fro-ing among their inhabitants, which were anything but self-contained, could still be well coordinated and dedicated to achieving ambitious common goals.

Economy and culture

Those who emphasise the village's isolation and ability to sustain itself can rightly point to the balance of resources that was planned when territorial boundaries were drawn before the Conquest or in some more remote period. When they were sited in valleys, for example, the townships or parishes ran up from the river or stream to the hills, incorporating meadow in the flood plain, arable on the valley floor, woodland on the slopes, and pasture on the highest ground. If a necessary type of land could not be included in the package in the immediate vicinity of the settlements, access was arranged at a distance, which usually consisted of a share in remote woodland or wood pasture, upland grazing, or a piece of meadow. In other words, peasants could obtain their corn, grazing, hay and litter for animals,

---

42. Field, 'Hampton Lovett', pp. 33–5.
43. K. French, *The People of the Parish. Community Life in a late Medieval Diocese* (Philadelphia, Pa., 2001); K. Farnhill, *Guilds and the Parish Community in Late Medieval East Anglia, c. 1470–1550* (York, 2001).

and timber, fuel and fencing material through their common rights somewhere within their village's territory.[44]

The landscapes that had developed by the thirteenth century, and often earlier, show many imbalances, with champion townships consisting predominantly of arable, with minimal quantities of meadow, or a complete absence of woodland. Often in the woodland landscapes cultivation had extended to provide the inhabitants with most of their basic supplies of cereals, but the areas of pastures and woods that remained were far too large for the subsistence needs of the inhabitants. The inequalities could be corrected by some non-commercial exchange, like the rights enjoyed by tenants in the Stour valley in south Warwickshire to obtain fuel and building timber from the woods at Lapworth in the Forest of Arden 16 miles to the north.[45]

The market was often the only means of acquiring these necessary resources. At Murcott in Watford in Northamptonshire, where the arable occupied virtually the whole of the township, in 1432–3 the lord of the manor bought timber and laths for repairs to a peasant house, at a cost of 14s. 4d., in the market town of Lutterworth.[46] When the villagers carried out their own repairs, which would have been the normal practice, they too would have bought the materials that were simply not available in the immediate locality. This observation can be extended to make the point that a range of everyday requirements of peasant holdings and households, such as some hay and litter for livestock, and foodstuffs for people, had to be purchased. Peasants from about 1200 had appreciated the advantages of specialisation in the rising market for the products that they could sell, such as grain and wool in the champion, and bacon, cattle, dairy products, timber and fuel in the woodlands. They were spurred on by the demand that rents and taxes be paid in cash, but also encouraged by the knowledge that at least some of the money that they gained from the market could be used to purchase goods and services. Peasant households bought foodstuffs, clothing, footwear, implements and utensils, according to peasant inventories, debt records and material remains from excavated houses. A husbandman from Holgate in Yorkshire, when he died in 1468, with relatively few possessions (he owned four horses, five cattle and a

---

44. C. S. and C. S. Orwin, *The Open Fields*, 3rd edn (Oxford, 1967), pp. 24–7; M. Gelling, *The West Midlands in the Early Middle Ages* (Leicester, 1992), pp. 13–14.
45. Warwickshire County Record Office, CR1911/1 (Lark Stoke miller given access to timber at Lapworth, 1376); Hollings, ed., *Red Book*, p. 292 (a statement of *c.* 1290 that as there was no wood or grove at Tredington, access was provided to woods at Blockley and Lapworth).
46. On Watford's topography and land use, D. Hall, 'Field systems and township structure', in M. Aston, D. Austin and C. Dyer, eds, *The Rural Settlements of Medieval England* (Oxford, 1989), pp. 196–204; Northamptonshire Record Office, Spencer MSS., roll 109 itemises the expenditure on buildings.

pig, and had 14 acres under crop), owed 2s. od. to a 'merchant', probably of nearby York, and 12d. to a smith, Thomas Garnet, together with sums of 2s. od., 5d. and 4d. to people whose occupations are not stated, but probably in each case for goods and services bought. He also owed 4s. 4d. in leasehold rent for his house. He lived near the city of York, and naturally bought goods there, but most peasants out in the country congregated on market day in the smaller towns.[47] All sections of village society were drawn into commerce, from the elite with 30-acre holdings who sold more than they purchased, to the cottagers who would have bought the daily necessities of grain and bread, and who would have regularly sought paid work beyond the confines of their own village. Villagers also imported labour, including skilled workers for buildings, as specialists such as carpenters and roofers were quite widely scattered, and at haymaking and harvest workers migrated over long distances, from town to country and from one region to another.[48]

Peasant involvement in markets helps to explain the points made earlier about landholding and migration. People regarded land not just as a source of subsistence for a family, but also as means of gaining a surplus of crops for sale, and appreciated that they could use land to raise cash, through both credit and the land market. This helped to weaken the ties between families and their holdings, in the commercialised regions, such as East Anglia, and in other parts of the country when land became less scarce after the demographic and social changes of the fourteenth century. The decision to move from one village to another, or from village to town, was taken in the light of country dwellers' experience of the market. Everyone, from those seeking employment to younger people finding a marriage partner, extending to wealthier neighbours acquiring land, were helped in their search by their familiarity with the roads that took them frequently out of their village, whether trudging or riding to a job, or delivering produce by cart to a local market town. The lack of economic self-sufficiency opened villages to outside contacts of every kind.

The inhabitants of late medieval villages were much involved in the internal business of their community, as any group of households could generate a rich mixture of neighbourly cooperation, intermarriages, alliances based on patronage and exchange of goods and labour, and they were also divided by disputes over access to scarce grazing, and by broken agreements, unpaid debts, antisocial behaviour, gossip, adulteries and petty violence. The manorial and church courts

47. Borthwick Institute of Historical Research, Dean and Chapter wills, 1468, Hall; C. Dyer, 'Small places with large consequences: the importance of small towns in England, 1000–1540', Hist. Research 75 (2002), pp. 15–17.
48. C. Dyer, An Age of Transition? Economy and Society in England in the Later Middle Ages (Oxford, 2005), pp. 226–8.

dealt with some of the conflicts, and although the lists of trespasses, debts, raisings of the hue and cry, petty thefts, assaults and gossiping give us no cause to be nostalgic for the peace and harmony of village life, nonetheless by their persistent naming of villagers as parties to the various disputes, and by attributing relatively few thefts or assaults to an 'unknown stranger', the records reinforce the impression of an enclosed and rather claustrophobic village community.

Nonetheless villagers were aware of a wider world, and outside influences had a major effect on their daily lives. In theory each village had some measure of autonomy, in the sense that locally agreed practices governed the agricultural routines, and many tenants held their land by the custom of the manor. Yet historians can only be impressed by the generic similarities between the rules and norms found in all villages. By-laws, setting out the rules for harvest employment, conditions for gleaning, prohibitions on carting corn by night or paying workers with sheaves, are found on many different manors over a number of midland counties.[49] They must have been spread by recommendation from one village to another, and most likely from peasant to peasant, because they often protected the community's interest rather than the lord's. The same reasoning can be applied to the diffusion of regulations governing social behaviour in the fifteenth century, such as those directed against hedge breaking, scolding and the playing of illicit games.[50] Changes in legal procedure, such as the growing reliance on juries to make decisions rather than the whole body of suitors, spread through the manor courts, presumably on the initiative of lords and their stewards.[51] The various borrowings from common-law practices, such as awareness of the legislation on land tenures at the end of the thirteenth century, or the adoption of joint tenancy for husbands and wives in the fourteenth, are likely to have originated with the stewards, but the court suitors (that is the peasants and especially the elite among them) acquired legal knowledge of their own, through their attendance at higher courts.[52]

Villagers knew about developments in national politics, and not just because the government sought to cultivate public opinion, as in the public statements issued during Edward III's war with France in the 1330s and 1340s.[53] The state awakened the political interest of the whole of society when it raised taxes directly

49. W. O. Ault, *Open Field Farming in Medieval England. A Study of Village By-Laws* (London, 1972).
50. M. K. McIntosh, *Controlling Misbehavior in England, 1370–1600* (Cambridge, 1998).
51. J. S. Beckerman, 'Procedural innovation and institutional change in the medieval manor court', *Law and Hist. Rev.* 10 (1992), pp. 197–212.
52. P. R. Hyams, 'What did Edwardian villagers mean by "law"?', in Razi and Smith, eds, *Medieval Society and the Manor Court*, pp. 69–116; R. M. Smith,' Coping with uncertainty: women's tenure in customary land in England, c. 1370–1430', in J. Kermode, ed., *Enterprise and Individuals in Fifteenth-Century England* (Stroud, 1991), pp. 43–67.
53. H. J. Hewitt, *The Organization of War under Edward III* (Manchester, 1966), pp. 158–65.

from the middling and better-off peasants, and when it legislated for improved law and order by requiring (in 1285) that each village set a watch by night. The popular concern for politics did not always follow the direction which the rulers preferred. When, like the people of Peatling Magna (Leicestershire) in 1265, peasants expressed their loyalty to the baronial reform movement which in their view acted for 'the welfare of the community of the realm', or when half a century later peasant opinion sympathised with Thomas Earl of Lancaster in his campaign against Edward II, they were showing their ability to criticise those in power, and to take the side of the aristocratic rebels.[54] Inaccurate rumour and apparently unfocused feelings of dissatisfaction were expressed by peasants, for example when the belief spread that Richard II was still alive in the early years of the fifteenth century, but they sometimes also had access to very precise information, as when the rebels of 1381 included in their list of 'traitors' some quite minor functionaries such as John Legge, who had proposed that the non-payment of the poll tax should be investigated.[55]

Material culture demonstrates the tendency of villagers to imitate their neighbours. Domestic architecture varied from one region to another, but the surviving peasant houses of the period 1380–1520 in a county such as Kent have a generic similarity in their design and construction, presumably reflecting the influence of local carpenters. The clients for whom the craftsmen worked must have preferred them to use styles resembling those in the villages and market towns of the vicinity.[56] A desire to keep up with developments in the wider world was expressed by churchwardens commissioning building work, who would sometimes visit other parishes to inspect a new structure, or in the case of the wardens of Helmingham in Suffolk, instructed the mason (who came from Norfolk) to build a church tower resembling Framsden in its overall dimensions, while the details, such as the door and windows, should be taken from Brandeston.[57] In some senses such commissions show villagers as conservatives, because they preferred tried and tested models. On the other hand, they evidently admired modernity, wishing their buildings to reflect the trends in fashion. In their choices of structures and fittings, churchwardens were also following wider

---

54. D. A. Carpenter, 'English peasants in politics, 1258–1267', *Past and Present* 136 (1992), pp. 3–42, especially p. 3; P. Schofield, *Peasant and Community in Medieval England 1200–1500* (Basingstoke, 2003), pp. 207–8.
55. S. Walker, 'Rumour, sedition and popular protest in the reign of Henry IV', *Past and Present* 166 (2000), pp. 31–65; R. H. Hilton, *Bondmen Made Free: Medieval Peasant Movements and the English Rising of 1381* (London, 1973), pp. 194–5.
56. S. Pearson, *The Medieval Houses of Kent: an Historical Analysis* (London, 1994)
57. L. F. Salzman, *Building in England down to 1540* (Oxford, 1967), pp. 547–9.

liturgical and theological developments. In this they no doubt learnt much from their own clergy, but again were acquiring ideas from their peers in other villages.

Conclusion

At no time can late medieval villages be described as 'self-contained', as the inhabitants needed to be in touch with the outside world where they could sell and buy. They shared in a common peasant culture, and kept in touch with national politics and religious changes.

In considering landholding and migration, within an overall picture of movement and change in the composition of the population, some qualifications are needed. Regional diversity meant that before 1349 midland villages experienced rather more continuity in landholding than those in East Anglia. After 1349, although midland peasants were more prone to movement, local differences can be noted between the champion villagers who migrated more readily, and the rather more stable dwellers in the woodlands. One thinks of the woodlands as more open and mobile, but their pastures and industries also offered better economic opportunities and encouraged people to remain. The social differences are clear, with a tendency for the better-off to stay, while cottagers, labourers and servants moved constantly. Females may have been prone to move, for employment and marriage. Migrants often did not move far, less than 20 miles, but even short journeys kept the village families in perpetual motion.

A handful of families survived for a number of generations, and helped to maintain knowledge of each village's customs. We can recognise the distinct social and economic 'character' of individual places over many centuries. No village, however, was an island, and it was not just the flow of people but also ideas that kept each place in constant communication with the outside world. In matters of production such as crop rotations and techniques of husbandry; in items of consumption such as houses and garments; and in less tangible concerns such as the latest saint's cult, the need for an Easter Sepulchre in the church, or the merits as rulers of the House of York, the villagers of the period 1250–1540 showed their familiarity with events far beyond the parish boundary.

2

Population mobility in rural Norfolk among landholders and others c.1440–c.1600

JANE WHITTLE

The Fussells, writing in 1953, evoked an image of rural society in early modern England with little or no population mobility, writing that 'many people in Tudor England were born in a village, lived in it all their lives, and died there without ever going farther, if as far, as the neighbouring village a couple of miles or so away.'[1] This picture of the self-contained village was shattered by Laslett's study of seventeenth-century Clayworth and Cogenhoe, first published in 1963. Comparing population listings, he found that the turnover of population was remarkably high. Discounting births and deaths, just over a third of the population in each community either arrived or left in a period of around a decade.[2] Subsequent work by researchers using church court depositions, which give information about length of residence, has confirmed this pattern across southern and midland England.[3] Studies of the late medieval land market also indicate a degree of mobility among the section of the population we might expect to be the most stable: those who held land.[4] However, our knowledge of landholding patterns remains poorly integrated into the growing literature on population mobility. This chapter uses evidence from church court depositions and manorial documents to compare wider patterns of mobility with those observable among landholders in Norfolk between the mid-fifteenth century and around 1600. It seeks to investigate

1. G. E. and K. R. Fussell, *The English Countrywoman* (reprinted, London, 1985), p. 17.
2. P. Laslett, 'Clayworth and Cogenhoe', in idem, *Family Life and Illicit Love in Earlier Generations* (Cambridge, 1977), p. 68. These two villages are located in Nottinghamshire and Northamptonshire respectively.
3. P. Clark, 'Migration in England during the late seventeenth and early eighteenth centuries', in P. Clark and D. Souden, eds, *Migration and Society in Early Modern England* (London, 1987), pp. 213–52.
4. P. D. A. Harvey, ed., *The Peasant Land Market in Medieval England* (Oxford, 1984); Z. Razi, 'The myth of the immutable English family', *Past and Present* 140 (1993), pp. 3–44; J. Whittle, 'Individualism and the family-land bond: a reassessment of land transfer patterns among the English peasantry', *Past and Present* 160 (1998) pp. 25–63.

Table 2.1 Geographical mobility in rural Norfolk, as recorded in church court depositions, 1499–1530

(a) Length of residence

	Men		Women	
	No.	%	No.	%
From birth	93	22.1	10	18.2
From 'youth'	38	9.0	–	0.0
50 years or more	5	1.2	1	1.8
40–9 years	22	5.2	2	3.6
30–9 years	19	4.5	3	5.5
20–9 years	65	15.4	9	16.4
10–19 years	67	15.9	15	27.3
5–9 years	49	11.6	5	9.1
1–4 years	51	12.1	9	16.4
Less than 1 year	12	2.9	1	1.8
Total	421	100	55	100

(b) Age at arrival

	Men		Women	
	No.	%	No.	%
Birth	93	22.6	10	18.2
'Youth'	38	9.2	–	0.0
0–10 years old	27	6.6	–	0.0
11–20 years old	64	15.6	10	18.2
21–30 years old	107	26.0	26	47.3
31–40 years old	55	13.4	4	7.3
41–50 years old	11	2.7	2	3.6
51–60 years old	14	3.4	3	5.5
61 or older	2	0.5	–	0.0
Total	411	100	55	100

Source: E.D. Stone, ed., Norwich Consistory Court Depositions 1499–1512 and 1518–30 (Norfolk Record Society 10, 1938). The sample includes Norfolk residents only and excludes clergymen and people dwelling in Norwich, Bishop's Lynn, Thetford and Great Yarmouth.

not only how many people moved, and how often, but why they moved, and whether some sections of the population were more mobile than others.

Table 2.1(a) shows the length of time deponents at the Norwich Consistory Court from rural Norfolk, between 1499 and 1530, had lived in their current place of residence. Only 22.1 per cent of men were resident since birth; others had made at least one move during their life. This is very similar to Poos's figure for late fifteenth-century Essex, 24.1 per cent, and Norfolk in the period 1660–1730, 21.5 per cent. A wider survey across southern and midland England for the period 1601–1710 found somewhat more stability, with 34.0 per cent of rural male deponents being 'lifetime-stayers'.[5] It seems clear that between the late fifteenth century and the early eighteenth century, only a minority of rural men lived in the village in which they had been born, and the population of eastern England was

5.   L. R. Poos, A Rural Society after the Black Death: Essex 1350–1525 (Cambridge, 1991), p. 170, tabulates all of these figures.

Table 2.2 The distance moved by bondmen and bondwomen from five manors in Norfolk, 1427–1556

Distance moved	No. of movements	% of movements
1–5 km	22	27.2
6–10 km	23	28.4
11–15 km	6	7.4
16–20 km	10	12.3
21–5 km	9	11.1
26–50 km	7	8.4
51–100 km	2	2.5
101 km +	2	2.5
Total	81	100

Sources: Norfolk Record Office (NRO), manorial records: Salle Kirkhall court book 1461–79 (NRS 2721 12D1) and court roll 1520–52 (NRS 2607 12B5); Hevingham (Bishops) court roll 1425–60 (NRS 19559 42D2); Hevingham Cattes court roll 1422–60 (NRS 14746 29D4), court roll 1425–9 (NRS 14755 29D4), court roll 1461–82 (NRS 14481 29C1) and court roll 1554–66 (NRS 14653 29D2); Saxthorpe Mickelhall court roll 1440–59 (NRS 19698 42E5) and court roll 1509–38 (NRS 19701 42E5); Saxthorpe Loundhall court roll 1422–59 (NRS 19670 42E2).

somewhat more mobile than that elsewhere. Church court depositions also usually state the age of the deponent, so it is also possible to calculate people's 'age at arrival': the age at which they settled in their current place of residence, as shown in Table 2.1(b). Most commonly men settled in their place of permanent residence in their twenties, although arrival in one's late teens or early thirties was also not unusual. Women appear to have been slightly more mobile than men, with only 18.2 per cent living in the place they were born, and settled down at a slightly younger age with a more pronounced concentration of movement in their teens and twenties. This pattern of mobility fits well with our wider picture of rural society in this period. Young people often left home in their late teens to work as servants, changing employer each year or so, until they left service to marry in their mid- to late twenties.[6] With marriage came the acquisition of land, or at least a place to live, and a more settled lifestyle.

Despite these high rates of mobility, there is general agreement that, on the whole, people did not move very far. Poos found that in fourteenth-century Essex, 'people moved, not aimlessly or randomly over long distances, but to and from communities within, typically, a radius of 10 to 15 miles.'[7] Evidence from Norfolk's mid-sixteenth-century quarter sessions courts relating specifically to servants shows that they rarely moved more than 20 miles between employers or

6. A. Kussmaul, *Servants in Husbandry in Early Modern England* (Cambridge, 1981); J. Whittle, *The Development of Agrarian Capitalism: Land and Labour in Norfolk 1440–1580* (Oxford, 2000), pp. 252–75; J. Whittle, 'Servants in rural England *c.* 1450–1650: hired work as a means of accumulating wealth and skills before marriage', in M. Agren and A. Erickson, eds, *The Marital Economy in Scandinavia and Britain 1400–1900* (Aldershot, 2005), pp. 89–107.
7. Poos, *A Rural Society*, p. 162.

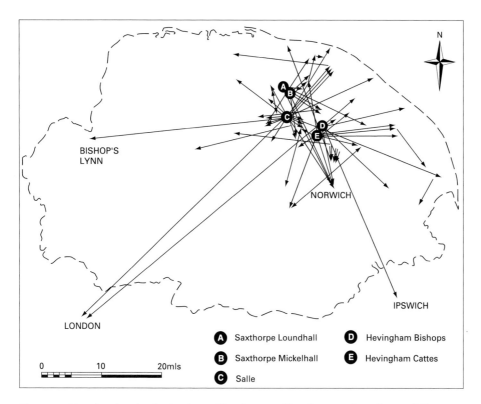

Figure 2.1 Map showing the destinations of bondmen and bondwomen from five Norfolk manors, 1427–1556 (Sources: see Table 2.2)

between home and employment,[8] a pattern confirmed by Kussmaul for the eighteenth century.[9] Manorial documents from Norfolk provide further evidence about the distances moved in the form of chevage payments. Many Norfolk manors in the fifteenth and early sixteenth centuries retained a system whereby people of hereditary unfree status (bondmen or bondwomen of blood) paid chevage fines to live away from the manor to which they belonged.

Table 2.2 and Figure 2.1 show the distances moved by unfree people from five north-east Norfolk manors in the period between 1427 and 1556. Eighty-one separate moves are recorded, the bulk of which occurred in the second half of the fifteenth century.[10] The great majority stayed within the region of north-east

8.   Whittle, *Agrarian Capitalism*, p. 273. Out of eighty-three cases, 37 per cent remained in the same settlement, 23 per cent moved to the neighbouring parish, only 2.4 per cent moved 20 miles or more within Norfolk, while another 2.4 per cent moved outside Norfolk. The other 35 per cent moved further than the neighbouring parish but less than 20 miles.

9.   Kussmaul, *Servants in Husbandry*, p. 57.

10. This distribution over time is caused by the nature of the documentation used, rather than any changing frequency of mobility.

Norfolk, although a few moved further afield. Most moves were local: 56 per cent went less than 10 kilometres (6.2 miles). Only eleven out of the eighty-one moves were over 25 kilometres (15.5 miles) in distance. Two individuals from different manors moved to London, while others moved to large towns in the region: Bishop's Lynn and Ipswich as well as Norwich.[11] Although they belonged to particular manors, these individuals were not necessarily landholders before or after they left the manor. We know some were young, because their ages are recorded, like the three sons of William atte Heithe of Salle, who in 1474 were aged fourteen, eleven and eight, and none of whom lived with their father. All lived quite close by, however, and two were living with relatives. Others displayed a pattern of high mobility that would accord with working as a servant or landless labourer. For instance William Gunware of Salle lived in four different places outside the manor between 1523 and 1533, moving every two or three years.[12] There were also cases of whole families moving. Thomas Howes of Hevingham Bishops and his five children moved to the neighbouring parish of Hainford in the 1440s. Thomas died in 1451, but in 1452 four of the children had moved to Horsham St Faith, another neighbouring parish, and were living there with one Robert Aldwyn, perhaps as a result of their mother's remarriage.

The accumulated evidence about geographical mobility in late medieval and early modern England has created a new orthodoxy among historians: the image of a highly mobile rural population. With this degree of movement it is hard to see villages as 'self-contained'. Yet a number of historians have argued that patterns of mobility differed between sections of the village population (in this book see pp. 14, 20, 86–93). Clark and Souden have concluded that 'more respectable members of local society tended to be less mobile than small craftsmen, servants and labourers'.[13] Nair confirms this pattern between 1550 and 1620 in her detailed study of Highley, Shropshire:

> there would appear to be two distinct types of life experience in the pre-enclosure community. Those who could obtain some land in Highley, even just the four or five acres that went with a cottage, tended to remain there all their married lives. Those who could not would seem to have been engaged in a series of moves every three or four years, or perhaps less, from village to village.[14]

In their study of Terling, Essex, Wrightson and Levine are more specific. Using

11.   There were six moves to Norwich.
12.   He lived in Mautby (1522, 1523), Bindham (1525), Mautby again (1527), Birlingham (1529, 1530, 1532), and Wickhampton (1533, 1534).
13.   P. Clark and D. Souden, 'Introduction', in Clark and Souden, eds, *Migration and Society*, p. 29.
14.   G. Nair, *Highley: The Development of a Community 1550–1880* (Oxford, 1988), pp. 57–8.

Figure 2.2 Saxthorpe Hall, Norfolk. The village of Saxthorpe was dominated by two manors, Saxthorpe Mickelhall and Saxthorpe Loundhall. Many tenants held land from both manors. This eighteenth-century house, now known as Saxthorpe Hall, was built on the site of Saxthorpe Loundhall manor (Photograph by Elizabeth Griffiths)

family reconstitutions gleaned from parish registers they found that between 1580 and 1699, persons in Category I, the gentlemen and great farmers of the parish, were the most fluid element in village society. The husbandmen and craftsmen in Category III were the most stable element. The experience of the yeomen of Category II lay somewhere between. In the case of the labouring poor of Category IV, however, we find that members of this group were subject to very rapid turnover prior to 1620.[15] Thus, to focus on landholders of non-gentry status and no great wealth is to search out the elements of stability in rural society.

The literature on tenants and landholding has a rather different historiography from that of more general population mobility. It uses manorial documents as its main source and has focused more on the land market and family–land bond, that

15. K. Wrightson and D. Levine, *Poverty and Piety in an English Village: Terling, 1525–1700* (Oxford, 1995), p. 81.

Table 2.3 Percentage of surnames surviving in forty-year intervals, 1440s–1636

Manor/data	1440s–1480s	1480s–1520s	Mid 16th cent.[1]	1593–1636
Kibworth Harcourt tenants	48.0	51.5	–	69.2
Hevingham Bishops tenants	26.2	27.8	32.8	–
Hevingham Bishops jurors	37.9	46.7	48.6	–
Saxthorpe Mickelhall jurors	27.3	43.5	42.3	–

Note:
1. The period covered for Hevingham Bishops was 1513–17 to 1553–7; for Saxthorpe Mickelhall 1540–4 to 1580–3.

Sources: C. Howell, *Land, Family and Inheritance in Transition. Kibworth Harcourt 1280–1700* (Cambridge, 1983), p. 249. Hevingham Bishops court rolls, NRO: 1425–60 (NRS 19559 42D2), 1483–5 (NRS 14763 29D4), 1485–1509 (NRS 19560 42D2), 1509–47 (NRS 13685 28D3), 1547–58 (NRS 14477 29C1) and miscellaneous roll (NRS 14487 29C1). Saxthorpe Mickelhall court rolls, NRO: 1440–59 (NRS 19698 42B2), 1463–82 (NRS 19699 42E5), 1483–1508 (NRS 19700 42E5), 1509–46 (NRS 19701 42E5), 1501, 1505 and 1538–61 (NRS 19702 42E5), 1547–58 (NRS 18583 33E2), 1560–76 (NRS 19703 42E6) and 1577–83 (NRS 19704 42E6).

is, the extent to which particular families held onto the same landholdings over time, rather than mobility per se, although studies of the land market and inheritance do shed light on the movement of people. Studies of continuity among manorial tenants have generally looked at the persistence of surnames over time, rather than studying individual histories. This approach is continued here, before closer attention is paid to individual histories towards the end of the chapter. Two manors were studied in some detail, Hevingham Bishops and Saxthorpe Mickelhall, both located in north-east Norfolk (Figure 2.2).

Although most of the data are drawn from manor court rolls and rentals, this is supplemented with information from other types of documents such as wills and parish registers to allow fuller family histories to be reconstructed. These data are used to make a number of comparisons. Norfolk had a particularly active land market: did this lead to a higher turnover of tenants than elsewhere in England?[16] To what extent did levels of turnover vary according to the amount of land held, and by types of tenure? How and why do the levels of mobility recorded among landholders vary from those observed using church court depositions and other sources?

Table 2.3 shows the percentage of tenant surnames that survive particular forty-year periods, that is, the proportion of the surnames belonging to those who held land at the start of the period that still appear among those who held land at the end of the period. It compares Kibworth Harcourt, Leicestershire, and the two

---

16. Whittle, 'Individualism', pp. 44–59.

Table 2.4 The persistence of surnames in Saxthorpe Mickelhall and Hevingham Bishops, Norfolk, 1440–1583

No. of years surname is present in manor	<5	5–30	31–60	61–90	>90	Sample size
Saxthorpe Mickelhall jurors 1440–1583	24.6%	40.2%	17.2%	9.8%	8.2%	122
Hevingham Bishops tenants 1444–1558	25.5%	47.8%	16.1%	6.6%	4.0%	274
Hevingham Bishops tenants who were also jurors 1444–1558	4.9%	46.6%	26.2%	14.6%	7.8%	103

Sources: Hevingham Bishops court rolls, NRO: 1425-60 (NRS 19559 42D2), 1483-5 (NRS 14763 29D4), 1485-1509 (NRS 19560 42D2), 1509-47 (NRS 13685 28D3), 1547-58 (NRS 14477 29C1) and miscellaneous roll (NRS 14487 29C1). Saxthorpe Mickelhall court rolls, NRO: 1440-59 (NRS 19698 42B2), 1463-82 (NRS 19699 42E5), 1483-1508 (NRS 19700 42E5), 1509-46 (NRS 19701 42E5), 1501, 1505 and 1538-61 (NRS 19702 42E5), 1547-58 (NRS 18583 33E2), 1560-76 (NRS 19703 42E6) and 1577-83 (NRS 19704 42E6).

Norfolk manors. The Norfolk evidence was collected in two ways. For Hevingham Bishops complete transcriptions of the court rolls were used, which allowed all the people holding land at any one time to be listed. However, not all tenants were resident. For this reason the turnover of manorial jurors was also examined. The cross-referencing of documents demonstrates that the juries of these two manors were made up of all male, resident tenants with customary land, excepting only gentlemen, clergy, and one or two tenants with very small pieces of land (2 acres or less) that was peripheral to the manor. For Saxthorpe Mickelhall the turnover of surnames among jurors was simply observed without reconstructing full landholding histories. It is clear that turnover was higher in the two Norfolk manors than in Kibworth Harcourt, although the difference was sharper in the mid-fifteenth century than in 1480–1520. In all cases turnover declined over time.

Table 2.4 presents the data from Hevingham Bishops and Saxthorpe Mickelhall in another form, showing how long particular surnames remained among a manor's jurors, tenants or tenants who were also jurors. Assuming the average amount of time for which one generation held land was approximately thirty years,[17] we can see that the majority of tenants held land for this time or less. Only a minority seem to have held land for two, three or more generations. However, the most transient category, those who were present for less than five years, was less likely to be well documented. When we combine those who held land and those who acted as a juror at Hevingham Bishops, and analyse the

17. Whittle, *Agrarian Capitalism*, p. 163.

Table 2.5 (a) Average length of residence of juror-tenant families in Saxthorpe Mickelhall manor who held land in 1500 (viewing a 144-year period from 1440 to 1583)

	Years	No. of juror-tenants
Overall	76.0	39
Those with less than 6 acres	72.4	10
Those with more than 20 acres	77.2	10
Those with freehold land	81.1	12
Those with customary land	74.5	23
Those with leasehold land	61.3	11
Those in families with no freehold land	61.6	16

(b) Average length of residence of tenant families in Hevingham Bishops manor who held land in 1509 (viewing a 115-year period from 1444 to 1558)

	Years	No. of tenants
Overall	62.4	52
Those with less than 6 acres	54.8	21
Those with more than 20 acres	67.3	8
Those with freehold land	65.4	8
Those families with no freehold land	58.1	39

Sources: Hevingham Bishops court rolls, NRO: 1425–60 (NRS 19559 42D2), 1483–5 (NRS 14763 29D4), 1485–1509 (NRS 19560 42D2), 1509–47 (NRS 13685 28D3), 1547–58 (NRS 14477 29C1) and miscellaneous roll (NRS 14487 29C1). Saxthorpe Mickelhall court rolls, NRO: 1440–59 (NRS 19698 42B2), 1463–82 (NRS 19699 42E5), 1483–1508 (NRS 19700 42E5), 1509–46 (NRS 19701 42E5), 1501, 1505 and 1538–61 (NRS 19702 42E5), 1547–58 (NRS 18583 33E2), 1560–76 (NRS 19703 42E6) and 1577–83 (NRS 19704 42E6). Saxthorpe Mickelhall rental NRO: 1500 (NRS19709 42E6), Hevingham Bishops rental NRO: 1509 (NRS 14759 29D4).

persistence of surnames, we find that only a very small percentage remained for less than five years. This is because some tenants held land only briefly (for instance, as part of complex land-transfer agreements, as heirs who quickly sold land, or as second husbands) and never became jurors. Likewise some jurors held that post only for a short period of time. Careers as jurors tended to be shorter than those as tenants, starting a few years after land was first acquired and ending a few years before the final surrender of land.

For this reason Table 2.5 focuses on juror-tenants: men who both held land and sat on the manorial jury. It takes a fixed point in time, in each case a list of tenants in a manorial rental, and examines how long those families remained as tenants in their respective manors. The averages are somewhat higher for Saxthorpe Mickelhall than Hevingham Bishops because a longer period of time is in view, 144 years rather than 115. If we retain the assumption that each generation was approximately thirty years, it seems that on average, particular families remained in residence for at least two generations, longer than is indicated by Table 2.4.

Figure 2.3 All Saints, Marsham, Norfolk. This church, serving the parish of Marsham, typifies the complexity of administrative and territorial arrangements in Norfolk. Many of the parishioners who built and used Marsham church, who were villagers of Marsham, held land from the manor of Hevingham Bishops. The church tower was built in the fourteenth century, but most of the visible work belongs to the fifteenth, the period of this study. Soon after 1500 the better-off parishioners, some of whom figure in this essay, arranged for the timber rood screen to be painted with figures of saints (Photograph by Elizabeth Griffiths)

Table 2.5 also shows comparisons between smallholders and larger tenants, and those holding land by different types of tenure. Those with more land were slightly more stable over time than those with smallholdings of less than 6 acres, although the differences are not dramatic. Some smallholding families did remain resident in a particular manor for long periods of time. The same is true for differences in tenure. Generally, tenants in eastern Norfolk held land by a combination of tenures. Freehold was the most favourable, almost equivalent to outright ownership, while leasehold gave tenants only limited, finite rights to the land. Families with freehold land were most likely to remain resident longest, and leaseholders least long, but again, the differences were not great. The effect was stronger in Saxthorpe where both leasehold and freehold were relatively plentiful.

Another contrast between Saxthorpe Mickelhall and Hevingham Bishops lay in the degree of their involvement in rural industry and craft-associated links with the Norwich. Hevingham Bishops lay within north-east Norfolk's rural worsted weaving region, while Saxthorpe Mickelhall lay outside it. Among apprenticeships enrolled with the Norwich Assembly between 1520 and 1620, there are twelve from the three parishes of Marsham, Hevingham and Brampton in Hevingham Bishops manor, but only three from the parishes of Saxthorpe and Corpusty in Saxthorpe Mickelhall manor.[18] (See Figure 2.3.)

Norwich apprenticeships are under-enumerated, as not all indentures detailed the apprentice's place of origin, and many apprenticeships seem not to have been enrolled. The villages in Hevingham Bishops manor had a larger population than those in Saxthorpe, but even taking this into account, Marsham, Hevingham and Brampton produced three times as many apprentices per person than Saxthorpe and Corpusty.[19] Hevingham Bishops manor was closer to the regional capital, 13 kilometres (8.1 miles) from the centre of Norwich compared to Saxthorpe Mickelhall's 24 kilometres (14.9 miles). Nonetheless, the most obvious explanation for the high number of Norwich apprentices leaving Hevingham Bishops was the presence of rural worsted weavers in this locality who had links with Norwich. Ten of the twelve apprentices from Hevingham went into worsted weaving compared to one out the three from Saxthorpe.

Patten's study of migration to East Anglian towns, which used apprenticeship indentures as a source, showed that the worsted weaving villages of north-east Norfolk typically sent above-average numbers of apprentices to Norwich in the

18. W. M. Rising and P. Millican, eds, *An Index of Indentures of Norwich Apprentices* (Norfolk Record Society 29, 1959).
19. Whittle, *Agrarian Capitalism*, p. 213.

sixteenth century.[20] This suggests that the presence of rural industry not only provided additional employment but also opened up the geographical horizons of rural communities. It may have served to strengthen the links between Hevingham Bishops manor, Norwich and London. Two Norwich aldermen held land in the manor in the early sixteenth century,[21] while Thomas Kesyng, a London mercer, lent money for mortgages, and as a result briefly held land in the manor in the 1480s. In contrast, Saxthorpe Mickelhall lay just outside the worsted weaving zone, and was more purely agricultural. Interestingly, these differences in outside links and occupational profiles do not seem to be reflected in the turnover of surnames among the tenants. Saxthorpe's tenant population was not any more stable than Hevingham's, and a comparison between craftsmen who held land and other tenants in Hevingham Bishops manor showed that craftsmen were no more mobile than other sections of the tenantry. Poos draws a similar conclusion on the strength of occupational evidence from fifteenth-century Essex church court depositions.[22]

Manorial studies have shown a distinct pattern of change over time. The proportion of land transferred between family members, an indication of the persistence of families in particular communities, was high in the period before the Black Death. Between the mid-fourteenth and mid-sixteenth centuries, mobility and discontinuity amongst landholders increased. But in the mid- to late sixteenth century, stability was regained, and the proportion of family land transfers increase once more.[23] For instance, 100 per cent of tenant surnames survived the period from 1280 to 1340 in Kibworth Harcourt, as they did again in 1636–79.[24] In Highley, Shropshire, between 1550 and 1590 rates were almost as high at 93.3 per cent.[25] Between the 1440s and the 1520s, the level of continuity in tenant surnames in Kibworth Harcourt was lower, as we have seen, and lower still in the two Norfolk manors. Even in Norfolk, however, there was a noticeable decline in the turnover of tenant surnames by the mid-sixteenth century, as shown in Table 2.3. Poos has argued that the impression of increased mobility after the Black Death is a mirage created by the documentation. Using evidence from Essex tithing lists he states that 'by the 1320s and 1330s … rural Essex communities

20. J. Patten, 'Patterns of migration and movement of labour to three pre-industrial East Anglian towns', in Clark and Souden, eds, *Migration and Society*, p. 82 and p. 91.
21. William Hert held land from 1496–1530 and Robert Harydauns from 1499–1514.
22. Whittle, 'Individualism', pp. 42–3; Poos, *A Rural Society*, p. 171. Unfortunately the Norfolk church court depositions do not give occupational details.
23. Whittle, 'Individualism', pp. 28–33.
24. C. Howell, *Land, Family and Inheritance in Transition. Kibworth Harcourt 1280–1700* (Cambridge, 1983), p. 242 and pp. 248–9.
25. Calculations from data in Nair, *Highley*, p. 56.

experienced rates of resident population turnover roughly equal in magnitude to those of English communities three hundred years later', and comparing levels of mobility shown by church court depositions he concludes 'it is striking ... how closely later-fifteenth-century Essex resembles East Anglia of two centuries later'.[26] There is a logical explanation for the higher turnover of tenants between the late fourteenth and early sixteenth centuries: low population levels combined with the leasing out of demesne land made land easier to acquire. Yet Poos's reading of evidence from church court depositions suggest that such changes over time in the landholding population caused barely a ripple in overall levels of mobility. Certainly, the comparison between mobility recorded in Norfolk's church court depositions of 1499–1530 and 1660–1730 given at the start of this chapter indicate virtually no change over time.[27]

While the evidence from church court depositions is not without problems, that from manorial documents, and Norfolk manors in particular, can be described as fragile at best. Comparison between these two sets of data requires awareness of three important differences: landholders were only one section of the population, manors are not the same as villages and surnames are not the same as individuals. Kibworth Harcourt and Highley were single-village manors: such manors are very rare in Norfolk. As we have seen, the men on the jury of Hevingham Bishops manor were drawn from three villages, Marsham, Hevingham and Brampton, while those of Saxthorpe Mickelhall came from five, Saxthorpe, Briston, Corpusty, Edgefield and Irmingland.[28] Some villages, such as Hevingham, were divided into more than one manor. Villages in eastern Norfolk are typically small and close together. The three villages in Hevingham Bishops were in a triangle roughly 3 kilometres (2 miles) apart. Saxthorpe, Corpusty and Irmingland were barely 1 kilometre apart, although Edgefield and Briston lay 4 and 5 kilometres away respectively. The form of manorial organisation, in itself, presents a challenge to the idea of a 'self-contained village'. Year after year men from neighbouring villages met and sat on a single manorial jury overseeing the transfer of land. This surely encouraged the exchange of information about land availability, especially as a number of these men also sat on the juries of other manors. This manorial structure has serious consequences for the measurement of mobility: the disappearance of a surname from a manor does not necessarily mean that that family had moved away from a village or ceased to hold land. For instance the Codenham family held land from Hevingham Bishops manor for over

---

26. Poos, A Rural Society, p. 160 and p. 170.
27. Although, obviously, changes may have occurred between 1530 and 1660.
28. This is evident by comparing court rolls with rentals and wills.

fifty years from 1456 to 1509. Yet taxation returns and wills show that the family remained resident and relatively prosperous in Hevingham until at least 1552, holding land from the manor of Hevingham Cattes.[29] This is surely one reason why the turnover of surnames appears so high on these manors, although it is not the whole explanation.

The relationship between the persistence of surnames and patterns of individual mobility is a complex one. The persistence of a surname among the tenants of a particular manor indicates a degree of continuity with land passing from generation to generation between close relatives. This in turn suggests the presence of 'lifetime stayers', people living in the manor in which they were born, although it is also possible that some left as young adults and returned later to take up land. However, continuity by this measurement requires only one heir with the same surname to remain in a particular manor in each generation: the majority of offspring could have moved elsewhere. On the other hand, the passage of land to or via a close female relative with a different surname produces an illusion of discontinuity. To relate the turnover of surnames to individual patterns of mobility it is necessary to examine inheritance strategies and the landholding histories of individuals. Inheritance patterns also suggest why some individuals in each generation moved from the place where they were born, providing some explanation for the patterns of mobility observed in rural England.

Table 2.6 shows the means by which tenants acquired land, their 'routes to landholding', in Hevingham Bishops manor.[30] It examines the history of three cohorts of tenants, each separated by roughly one generation. Route A was the classic route of inheriting land from a close relative. Routes B and C involved the transfer of land to or from women, while D notes family links via a daughter although not necessarily the transfer of land across that link. Routes E, F and G all involved the acquisition of land from non-relatives. The custom of inheritance in Hevingham manor was impartible, was the land passing to one son. Wills and death-bed land transfers were frequently used to overrule custom, but most commonly land still passed to a single son. Some families, such as the Bisshops, achieved long-term continuity by passing land by route A. We can trace the passage of land through five generations of the Bisshop family in this way, from John Bisshop to his son Robert in 1484, from Robert to his nephew Robert in 1500, to his son Edmund in 1556, and to his son, another Robert in 1573. On some

---

29. The will of Robert Codnam, husbandman, 1552, shows that the land then passed to his daughter Margaret Bisshop and her two sons.
30. An earlier version of this table appears in Whittle, *Agrarian Capitalism*, p. 161. Here data for 1573 have been added.

Table 2.6 Routes to landholding in Hevingham Bishops manor, comparing the tenants of 1509, 1540 and 1573

Year	1509		1540		1573	
	N	%	N	%	N	%
A	18	32.7	18	35.3	17	42.5
B	6	10.9	5	9.8	1	2.5
C	3	5.4	5	9.8	3	7.5
D	1	1.8	2	3.9	1	2.5
E	6	10.9	3	5.9	4	10.0
F	4	7.3	6	11.8	2	5.0
G	13	23.6	2	23.5	10	25.0
H	4	7.3	0	0.0	2	5.0
No. of tenants	55	100	51	100	40	100

Key to landholding routes:
A. Received land from parent or other close relative.
B. Widow of tenant.
C. Married widow of tenant.
D. Married a daughter of tenant (although did not necessarily receive land from her parents).
E. Acquired land from non-relative, but father was tenant of manor.
F. Appeared in manor and some years later acquired land, no known previous connections.
G. Appeared first acquiring land, no known previous connections with manor.
H. Unknown (cannot be traced due to gaps in court rolls).
Sources: Hevingham Bishops court rolls, NRO: 1425–60 (NRS 19559 42D2), 1483–5 (NRS 14763 29D4), 1485–1509 (NRS 19560 42D2), 1509–47 (NRS 13685 28D3), 1547–58 (NRS 14477 29C1) and miscellaneous roll (NRS 14487 29C1), with the addition of 1509 rental (NRS 14759 29D4), rough court book 1564-72 (NRS 12945 27F2), rough court book 1573-82 with 1573 rental (NRS 13716 28D6), wills from Marsham, Hevingham and Brampton, and Marsham parish register 1538-56: all NRO.

occasions landholdings were split between heirs, as in the case of the long-lived William Mollet, who on his death in 1550 divided his landholding between his son and three grandsons.[31] Two of the grandsons were still tenants in 1573. Despite this degree of continuity, most generations of particular families produced a number of children who did not inherit land or settle in the parish in which they were born. The reconstruction of inheritance patterns in Hevingham Bishops for the period 1440–1579 using manorial records and wills found that while 42 per cent of sons received land from a close relative, and a further 9 per cent managed to acquire land by other means in their place of birth, 49 per cent moved away from the manor.[32] This suggests considerable stability among tenants' sons, with 51 per cent settling in their place of birth, compared to a figure of 22 per cent of rural males being 'lifetime-stayers' from Norfolk's church court depositions.

Daughters are more difficult to trace. North-east Norfolk wills record that only 6 per cent of daughters or their husbands received land from the daughter's father.[33] This picture is confirmed in Table 2.6. In all three cohorts the only

31. William Mollet first acquired land in 1495, and inherited a holding from his father in 1508.
32. Whittle, *Agrarian Capitalism*, p. 158, based on the histories of sixty-seven sons.
33. Ibid., p. 153.

non-married women holding land were widows. There were four cases of daughters of tenants settling in the manor with their husbands: in two cases they did receive some land from the daughter's family, but in the other two land was purchased from non-relatives.[34] Widows with land are easier to trace with manorial documents and wills, and often moved with remarriage.[35] For instance Avice Pye/Wilson/Pynnyng/Lombe lived with her first husband in the village of Erpingham a few kilometres to the north of Hevingham, her second husband is untraceable, while her third, Edmund Pynnyng, was a tenant of Hevingham Bishops resident in Marsham. Her last husband came from the neighbouring market town of Cawston, but seems to have moved to Marsham to help Avice manage the landholding left to her by Pynnyng. On her death in 1558 Avice passed this land to her grandson by her first marriage, thus introducing a new surname into the manor. The grandson, Richard Pye, appears as a tenant in 1573.

In most cases, however, when a new surname appeared in the manor, no connection could be traced to previous tenants (Routes F and G). Despite an increased importance in family land transfers as a means of acquiring land over the sixteenth century, men who purchased land and had no previous connection with the manor still made up 30 per cent of tenants in 1573. Thus, the other side of the coin which saw nearly half of tenants' sons disappear before acquiring land was the appearance of non-inheriting sons from other manors. Categories F and G are separated in Table 2.6 because it seemed of some interest that a number of these men were evidently resident in the manor, perhaps working as servants or living as subtenants, for some years before they managed to acquire land held directly from the manor. Men following Routes F and G held their land for less long than men who acquired land from relatives, 21.8 years rather than 37.7.[36] As similar proportions in each group surrendered land due to death, the most likely cause of this difference was that Routes F and G meant land was acquired somewhat later in life than Route A, as these men needed time to accumulate the necessary wealth to purchase land and find a suitable landholding.[37] When the life histories of twenty-five Hevingham tenants were reconstructed it was found that those who purchased their main landholding from a non-relative, did so between the ages of twenty and thirty-nine, while those who inherited land did so between

34. For other studies of marriage, courtship and mobility see, D. O'Hara, *Courtship and Constraint: Rethinking the Making of Marriage in Tudor England* (Manchester, 2000), pp. 122–36.

35. J. Whittle, 'Inheritance, marriage, widowhood and remarriage: a comparative perspective on women and landholding in north-east Norfolk, 1440–1580', *Continuity and Change* 13 (1998), pp. 59–63.

36. This refers to 1509 cohort only.

37. Whittle, *Agrarian Capitalism*, p. 163.

the ages of fourteen and forty-four reflecting the fact that inheritance was dependent on their father's death. However, sons waiting for their inheritance generally acquired at least some land at an earlier age, in anticipation of their inheritance. This, in part, explains the spread of 'age at arrival' found in the church court data shown in Table 2.1 (b).

In conclusion, it is unsurprising that manorial records show a pattern of mobility different from that depicted in church court depositions: manorial documents record a smaller, and evidently less mobile, section of society. Church court depositions show that the most mobile phase of the lifecycle was between the ages of fifteen and thirty. The end of this period of mobility coincided with the acquisition of property. Most landholders were over thirty years in age. There was a higher turnover of surnames among landholders in the fifteenth and early sixteenth century than there was in earlier or later periods. The easy availability of land meant sons were less likely to acquire a holding and settle in the place where they were born: there was no need to wait for their father's death and to inherit, if land could be easily acquired elsewhere. Whether this encouraged or discouraged mobility over an individual's lifetime remains to be tested. Easy availability of property might have encouraged repeated moves, but on the other hand, men may have acquired land at a younger age and remained as tenants in one place for longer.

Regional differences in the turnover of tenant families are partly due to problems with documentation: the complex manorial structures found in Norfolk inflate the impression of population mobility. But it seems likely there were also real differences. Manors such as Kibworth Harcourt and Highley did not have the type of active or flexible land markets that allowed newcomers to establish themselves easily, if they had the necessary financial resources: Hevingham Bishops and Saxthorpe Mickelhall did.[38] Regional differences in mobility are evident in church court depositions (although from a later date), as well as manorial documents: Clark found that the proportion of lifetime-stayers among rural males in Oxfordshire and Gloucestershire respectively was 41.6 per cent and 54.1 per cent, compared to 21.5 per cent in Norfolk.[39] It seems that forms of land tenure could affect levels of mobility among landholders. But there was some stability even in these Norfolk villages: tenants and their families were considerably less mobile than the population as a whole. Once men acquired land they typically held it for over twenty years, and in the sixteenth century around half of all sons became landowners in the same manor as their father and settled in the place where they were born. Even in Norfolk it is easy to find examples of families

38. Whittle, 'Individualism', pp. 49–59.
39. Clark, 'Migration in England', p. 221. This relates to the period 1660–1730.

which remained resident in the same village for a century or more. Given that Norfolk villages were quite small, these more permanent families must have loomed large for contemporaries, as they do for the historian of manorial records, giving an impression of stability despite high levels of mobility.

3

Destitution, liminality and belonging: the church porch and the politics of settlement in English rural communities, c.1590–1660

STEVE HINDLE

The nature and extent of the loops of association that bound together the people of rural England in the past have long been controversial among historians. Two paradigms have tended to dominate the scholarship.[1] On the one hand, it is argued, vertical ties of paternalism, deference and subordination entwined groups of individuals of varying social status whose primary affiliation lay with the local community, usually understood not as the village (a unit of residence) but as the parish (a unit of obligation and control).[2] (For problems of definition, see pp. 3–5 above). On the other, it has been suggested, the development of horizontal allegiances borne of the shared experience of 'bearing rule' (among the gentry), of farming for the market (among the middling sort), or of wage labour (among the poorer sort) encouraged the formation of a socially stratified, geographically extensive class consciousness.[3] Historians have broadly agreed that there has been over time a transition in rural society from the solidarities of community to those of class, though the timing, extent and finality of that process remain highly controversial. These are, of course, complex issues which have a resonance far beyond the immediate concerns either of this essay or of the collection in which it appears. It is nonetheless significant that very recent contributions to this aspect of the 'transition debate' have reversed the conventional polarities. From one perspective, early modernists have begun to rehabilitate class as a legitimate idiom of social description for the identities shared by plebeian social groups in the

1. D. Underdown, 'Community and class: theories of local politics in the English Revolution', in B. C. Malament, ed., *After the Reformation: Essays in Honour of J. H. Hexter* (Manchester, 1980), pp. 147–65, provides an interesting account of the relationship between these two traditions in the historiography of seventeenth-century England.
2. S. Hindle, 'A sense of place? Becoming and belonging in the rural parish, 1550–1650', in A. Shepard and P. Withington, eds, *Communities in Early Modern England* (Manchester, 2000), pp. 96–114.
3. E. Thompson, *The Making of the English Working Class* (London, 1963); M. Reed and R. Wells, eds, *Class, Conflict and Protest in the English Countryside, 1700–1880* (London, 1990).

seventeenth century. The cloth-workers and coalminers who have featured so prominently in recent historical writing, it is argued, developed and revelled in a collective consciousness which expanded well beyond their local communities and extended through regional and national markets for labour and goods.[4] From another perspective, however, modern historians have explained the attenuation of that class consciousness by emphasising the enduring primacy of parochial identity well into the nineteenth century. 'Local xenophobia', it has been suggested, actively restrained the formation of a working class in rural England.[5]

It is, therefore, a particularly interesting time to be thinking about the relationship between class and community in the English village. As Keith Wrightson has noted, even within the local community there was both a 'hierarchy' *and* a 'continuum' of belonging.[6] Wrightson's important insight nonetheless begs further questions: how extensive was that continuum?; and how and where did it intersect with hierarchy? What was the relationship between the identities crystallised in the sense of belonging to a particular place and those born of the recognition of wider affinities woven in networks of production, distribution and exchange? This essay takes very seriously Keith Snell's emphasis on the extent to which the social horizons of working people were 'limited by the parish bounds'.[7] But it is concerned rather with the origins, development and reinforcement of that local consciousness than with its undoubted longevity. If, as Snell suggests, the poor law was one factor (among many) that helped to sustain highly localised loyalties and antagonisms at the end of the nineteenth century, it is imperative to explore the extent to which the poor law bolstered, or perhaps even created, them at the beginning of the seventeenth. This essay is an attempt to do just that, by exploring the impact of early poor-law policy on the extent to which the villagers of sixteenth and seventeenth century England identified themselves primarily, though never of course exclusively, with the parish.

In considering the 'self-contained' village in the sixteenth and seventeenth centuries it will be suggested that rural communities were, if anything, rather less open to migration in late Elizabethan and Stuart England either than they had

---

4. A. Wood, *The Politics of Social Conflict: The Peak Country, 1520–1770* (Cambridge, 1999), pp. 10–26, 316–25; J. Walter, *Understanding Popular Violence in the English Revolution: The Colchester Plunderers* (Cambridge, 1999), Chapter 7 ('Cloth and class'), esp. pp. 260–84; D. Rollison, 'Discourse and class struggle: the politics of industry in early modern England', *Social Hist.* 26 (2001), pp. 166–89; K. Wrightson, ' "Those which be participant of the common wealth": class, governance and social identities in early modern England' (unpublished paper).
5. K. D. M. Snell, 'The culture of local xenophobia', *Social Hist.* 28 (2003), pp. 1–30.
6. K. Wrightson, 'The politics of the parish in early modern England', in P. Griffiths, A. Fox and S. Hindle, eds, *The Experience of Authority in Early Modern England* (London, 1996), p. 19.
7. Snell, 'The culture of local xenophobia', p. 1.

been in the medieval period or than they were to become in the eighteenth century. Given the high degree of incorporation that had long characterised the English polity, it is axiomatic that villagers were subsumed within larger matrices of governance, of exchange and of belief. Although, as Christopher Dyer's contribution to this collection suggests, the permeability of the medieval rural community cannot be taken entirely for granted, he nonetheless argues that 'at no time can late medieval villages be described as "self-contained", not least because the inhabitants needed to be in touch with the outside world where they could sell and buy'.[8] The more interesting issue for historians of the early modern period who enjoy access to qualitative evidence superior to that available to medievalists, is the identification of the thresholds of *belonging* in the village community. One obvious possibility of such a threshold is the parish boundary, popular consciousness of which was reinforced by the rituals of rogationtide, during which the bounds of the local community were perambulated.[9] The single mothers carted across the parish boundary to ensure that they bore their bastards as a charge to the ratepayers of another community could provide eloquent testimony of the extent to which the actions of parish officers embodied, perhaps even enforced, the popular 'sense of place' encouraged on 'gang' days. Parish boundaries were, nonetheless, easily crossed, and this essay is less concerned with the policing of geographical thresholds than with the fate of those poor migrants who traversed them. Indeed, it takes as its focus a social site at the very heart of the local community, a symbolic space in which marginal people might seek the charity of the local community. The church porch, I want to suggest, was a particularly significant arena for the negotiation of belonging to the rural community, and its liminal associations ensured that the destitute favoured it as a space in which they might advertise their plight.

Points of entry

In July 1634, the justices of the peace of north-east Norfolk investigated the nature and scale of destitution in a number of villages in the hundred of Taverham. In a chapter of sad stories – of 'exceeding pore' men, their wives and children 'like to lie in the streete' – perhaps the saddest is that of Robert Greene of Sprowston. Greene had offered houseroom 'in case of necessity' to his destitute sister, recently widowed, who had returned to the parish. Because the ratepayers (and the

---

8.   Dyer, 'Were late medieval villages "self-contained"?', above, p. 27.
9.   Rogation still awaits its historian, but for suggestive comments see D. Underdown, *Revel, Riot and Rebellion: Popular Politics and Culture in England, 1603–1660* (Oxford, 1985), pp. 14, 45–7, 81, 90–1; Hindle, 'A sense of place?', pp. 107–8; D. Fletcher, 'The parish boundary: a social phenomenon in Hanoverian England', *Rural Hist.* 14 (2003), pp. 177–96.

Figure 3.1 The half-timbered south porch of St John's Berkswell (Warwickshire). Built in the sixteenth century, the upper storey is a cottage-like chamber which originally served as the village school (www.heart-of-england.net)

overseers of the poor who represented their financial interests) feared that her family might become chargeable to the parish, however, Greene was told to evict them, with the result that a single mother and her four children had nowhere to go, and were forced to take shelter in the porch of Sprowston parish church.[10]

Widow Greene's predicament raises three questions, to which the following discussion seeks answers: first, what kind of physical environment was the church porch?; second, how commonly did the destitute seek refuge there?; and third, and more significantly for our purposes, why did they choose this, above all other

10. TNA:PRO, SP16/272/44 (the justices of the peace of Taverham, Norfolk, to the privy council, 22 July 1634). The four villages concerned are Beeston, Felthorpe, Hainford and Sprowston.

spaces, as a place in which they might seek shelter? To turn, first, to the physical experience of squatting in the church porch, it is immediately obvious that the architecture of this particular 'room' might vary considerably between parishes, if indeed the church had one at all. From the later Middle Ages well into the sixteenth (and very occasionally even into the seventeenth) century, large sums were lavished upon the porches of some churches, which along with the tower, were among the most visible parts of the fabric.[11]

At Yatton (Somerset), for example, the south porch was rebuilt in the 1450s on the proceeds of parish ales. The patrons of the Hertfordshire parishes of Bushey and Broxborne rebuilt their porches as late as the 1630s.[12] There were occasionally lofts or chambers above church porches, as at Berkswell (Warwickshire) (see Figure 3.1), Walberswick (Suffolk), St Edmund (Salisbury), Ludlow (Shropshire), Bishop's Cleeve (Gloucestershire), Bredon (Worcestershire) or Breamore (Hampshire).[13] The roof might be richly decorated or carved, and it was not unknown for porches, as at All Saints Evesham, to have roof bosses that communicated the symbolism of the Passion to those who raised their eyes to heaven.[14] Less durable timber-framed porches were also frequently added to churches in the late Middle Ages and were occasionally (like that at Otford, Kent in 1637), built even in the seventeenth century, though it is possible that several original wooden porches of this type may have been removed in recent times.[15]

Most church porches were, however, single-storey stone-built affairs, lined with benches and sometimes illuminated by small windows. Although a heavy oaken door would divide this rectangular chamber from the nave, the porch lay open to the churchyard on the other side, and all and sundry, including the vagrant and the destitute, might easily secure access. (Many of the insubstantial outer doors, principally designed to keep out birds, which enclose porches in the twenty-first century are of very recent construction.) Although some, such as

11. On the architecture and significance of the church porch, see N. J. G. Pounds, *A History of the English Parish: The Culture of Religion from Augustine to Victoria* (Cambridge, 2000), pp. 387–8.
12. K. L. French, *The People of the Parish: Community Life in a Late Medieval English Diocese* (Philadelphia, Pa., 2003), pp. 136, 152, 160; C. Platt, *The Parish Churches of Medieval England* (London, 1981), p. 97; P. M. Hunneyball, *Architecture and Image-Building in Seventeenth-Century Hertfordshire* (Oxford, 2004), pp. 139–40.
13. J. C. Cox, *Churchwardens' Accounts from the Fourteenth Century to the Close of the Seventeenth Century* (London, 1913), pp. 23, 75, 85; J. P. McAleer, 'The rooms over the porches of Bishop's Cleeve and Bredon parish churches: a question of dating', *Trans. Bristol and Glos. Arch. Soc.* 120 (2002), pp. 133–75; W. Rodwell and E. C. Rouse, 'The Anglo-Saxon rood and other features in the south porch of St Mary's Church, Breamore, Hampshire', *Antiquaries Jnl* 64 (1984), pp. 298–325.
14. C. J. P. Cave, 'All Saints Church, Evesham: the wooden boss in the porch', *Trans. Worcs. Arch. Soc.* ns 16 (1940 for 1939), pp. 57–8.
15. T. P. Smith, 'Three medieval timber-framed church porches in West Kent: Fawkham, Kemsing and Shoreham', *Archaeologia Cantiana* 101 (1985 for 1984), esp. p. 139.

Figure 3.2 Door leading to the mid-thirteenth-century church porch in the west tower of St Peter's, Kineton (Warwickshire), where James Clarke, his wife and child lodged in the winter of 1634–5

Warborough (Oxfordshire) for example, had stout outer doors secured with locks and keys, the shelter provided by the typical church porch was inadequate by any reasonable standards of warmth and comfort.[16] It was not, accordingly, unknown for the destitute to be found dead (of cold, perhaps even of hunger) in church porches, as they were at Minchinhampton (Gloucestershire) in 1598 or Brewood (Staffordshire) in 1621.[17] It is equally possible that a high proportion of the occasional 'poor strangers' for whom parish officers provided burials had also perished in the church porch.[18] There was an obvious temptation for the destitute

16. S. A. Peyton, ed., *Churchwardens' Presentments in the Oxfordshire Peculiars of Dorchester, Thame and Banbury* (Oxfordshire Rec. Soc., 10, 1928), p. 96.
17. J. Bruce, 'Extracts from the accounts of the churchwardens of Minchinhampton in the county of Gloucester', *Archaeologia* 35 (1853), p. 437; D. M. Palliser, 'Dearth and disease in Staffordshire, 1540–1670', in C. W. Chalkin and M. A. Havinden, eds, *Rural Change and Urban Growth, 1500–1800* (London, 1974), p. 64.
18. See, for example, the half-dozen cases recorded for Cowden (Kent) 1611–46 in E. Turner, 'Ancient parochial account book of Cowden', *Sussex Arch. Collections*, 20 (1882), pp. 99, 101, 103, 106.

to build campfires there, as they did at King's Sutton (Northamptonshire) in 1612 or at Kettleby (Leicestershire) in 1637, though this tactic was obviously downright hazardous in those porches that were built of wood.[19]

Given the obvious discomforts and risks, it is all the more surprising that Widow Greene and her children were certainly not unique in taking refuge in the church porch of a rural community in this period. Her tactic was imitated by 'Old Scott' in King's Sutton (Northamptonshire) in 1612; by James Clarke, his wife and child at Kineton (Warwickshire) (Figure 3.2) in 1634; and by John Salter and his pregnant wife Isabel, and William Loasby 'in his extreme need and wanting a lodging', in the Leicestershire villages of Sileby and Kettleby respectively, both in 1637. To these could be added Sarah Woodfall and her five children at Napton-on-the-Hill (Warwickshire) in 1650; William Round at Avon Dassett (Warwickshire) in 1655; Daniel Smith and his heavily pregnant wife at Frankton (Warwickshire) in 1655; John Woods, his wife and seven-week-old child in Ingworth (Norfolk) in 1665; Susannah Russell at Southam (Warwickshire) in 1674; John Rivett and his family at Sisland (Norfolk) in 1676; and William Titmouse, his wife and two children at Wallington (Hertfordshire) in 1682. All these individuals claimed to be homeless, and chose to publicise their destitution by camping out, sometimes for weeks at a time, in the porch of a parish church. Some of them, doubtless, strategically chose large churches in relatively wealthy parishes; others simply took advantage of the nearest available shelter.[20]

It may even be the case, as Keith Thomas once suggested, that the settled and vagrant poor alike felt that they had a customary right 'to sleep in the church if they had no other accommodation'. In 1637, indeed, the inhabitants of one Leicestershire parish referred almost instinctively to the church porch as the place 'where the beggars do usually lie'.[21] Some of those who did so were evidently vagrants, who frequently occupied church porches to take shelter and solicit alms, as did a Lincolnshire vagabond in Norwich at Christmas 1553; 'two beggar women' in Crowle (Worcestershire) in 1633; and an escaped felon in Leyton

19. Peyton, ed., *Churchwardens' Presentments*, p. 290; Leicestershire Record Office (hereafter LRO), 1D/41/13/64, fo. 258ᵛ.
20. Peyton, ed., *Churchwardens' Presentments*, pp. 287, 290; S. C. Ratcliff, H. C. Johnson and N. J. Williams, eds, *Warwick County Records*, 9 vols (Warwick, 1935–64), Vol. I, pp. 190–1; Vol. III, pp. 38, 258, 261; Vol. VII, p. 21; B. Capp, 'Life, love and litigation: Sileby in the 1630s', *Past and Present* 154 (2004), p. 69; LRO, 1D/41/13/64, fo. 258ᵛ; J. M. Rosenheim, ed., *The Notebook of Robert Doughty, 1662–1665* (Norfolk Rec. Soc., 54, 1989), p. 61; Norfolk Record Office, C/S2/3, unfol. (October 1676); W. Le Hardy, ed., *Hertford County Records*, 9 vols (Hertford, 1905–39), Vol. VI, p. 355.
21. K. Thomas, *Religion and the Decline of Magic: Studies in Popular Belief in the Sixteenth and Seventeenth Centuries* (London, 1971), p. 562; Capp, 'Life, love and litigation', p. 69.

(Essex) in 1671.[22] In one instance, indeed, the churchwardens of Warborough (Oxfordshire) actually colluded with a beggar by giving him the key to the church porch, a gesture of charity that doubtless infuriated the ratepayers.[23] Church porches were among the numerous lodging places associated with beggary by the Norwich city fathers in their 'orders for the poor' of 1571; and vagrants were occasionally apprehended in the porches of Leicestershire, Somerset and Wiltshire parishes into the seventeenth century.[24] As the case of Widow Greene suggests, however, vagrants enjoyed no monopoly on destitution, which was a fate sometimes visited on poor migrants and perhaps even on ancient settled members of the local community.

Destitute men and women in early modern England doubtless slept anywhere they could: in barns and outhouses, perhaps, maybe even under hedges or beneath oak trees. The symbolic significance of Widow Greene's choice of the church porch for her temporary accommodation should not, therefore, be underestimated. The church porch was, after all, not only a very public space, it was also a liminal one, the symbolic threshold of belonging to the parish. It had long enjoyed various liturgical functions: it was the place at which (during the marriage service) young men and women had customarily been admitted into full adult membership of the local community; the place in which those delinquent members of the congregation who were excluded from communion were usually made to wait while they prepared to perform public penance; the place from which women had traditionally processed as they were reassimilated into the community during the churching ritual.[25] It was also a focus of popular superstitions associated with death and the afterlife. The 'church porch watch' was a vigil practised throughout England, but especially in the northern counties, from at least the seventeenth long into the nineteenth century. On St Mark's Eve (24 April) or some other major calendrical festival, semi-professional seers, minor church officials, those living or working near the church, or even young thrill-seekers, would spend the night sitting in the porch to see the ghosts or shades of those

22. W. Rye, ed., 'Depositions taken before the Mayor and Aldermen of Norwich, 1549–1567', *Norfolk Arch.*, 1 (1905), p. 54; Worcestershire Record Office, QSR1/1/58/71; J. A. Sharpe, ed., '*William Holcroft His Booke*': *Local Office-Holding in Late Stuart Essex* (Essex Historical Documents 2, 1986), p. 60.
23. Peyton, ed., *Churchwardens' Presentments*, p. 96.
24. R. H. Tawney and E. Power, eds, *Tudor Economic Documents*, 3 vols (London, 1924), Vol. II, p. 317; A. L. Beier, *Masterless Men: The Vagrancy Problem in England, 1560–1640* (London, 1985), pp. 83, 223.
25. For marriage, see C. Brooke, *The Medieval Idea of Marriage* (Cambridge, 1989), pp. 248–50; D. Cressy, *Birth, Marriage and Death: Ritual, Religion and the Life-Cycle in Tudor and Stuart England* (Oxford, 1997), p. 336; for penance, see D. Postles, 'Penance and the market place: a reformation dialogue with the medieval church (c. 1250-c. 1600)', *Jnl of Ecclesiastical Hist.* 54 (2003), pp. 441–68; for churching, see Cressy, *Birth, Marriage and Death*, pp. 205–6.

destined to die during the coming year. As Samuel Menefee has noted, the temporal and physical location of the ritual marked the boundaries between the natural and the supernatural, between the sanctified church and the everyday world. Several of the various tale-motifs associated with the watch – the correct prediction of another's death, the prediction of death in response to a complaint, and the fulfilment of unusual predictions – resonate with the tradition that the poor or subordinate might censure, perhaps even curse, their betters for their hard-heartedness.[26] Little wonder that beggars, like penitents, should stand in the porch seeking worldly or otherworldly salvation.

The Reformation abrogated many of these rituals and purified others, sometimes removing them from the margins to the body of the church. Over time, it seems, the functions of the church porch became increasingly secular. In 1599, the parishioners of St Alphage, London Wall contemplated building a vestry house in the church porch. In the early 1620s, remembered John Evelyn, children as young as four were taught the rudiments of reading and writing 'in the church porch' of the parish of Wotton (Surrey). By the middle of the seventeenth century, the Essex magistracy was insisting that putative fathers of bastard children made payments specified by paternity orders in the church porch of the appropriate parish.[27] This is not to deny that the porch had been a site of secular activity in the period before the Reformation: cloth had been sold in the porch of St Michael's Coventry, for instance, until the town leet forbade it in 1456.[28] Porches doubtless served as an arena for the holding of conversations and the sealing of bargains across the medieval and early modern periods.

The popular perception of the porch as a place where belonging was defined was nonetheless probably enduring, and was almost certainly reinforced by the fact that the charity of the parish was frequently distributed there to those considered deserving, weekly after Sunday sermons in the case of pensions or collections, biannually at the major festivals of the church calendar in the case of doles.[29] Little wonder, therefore, that when the poor sought to chastise the propertied for their lack of charity, they chose the church porch as the most

26. S. P. Menefee, 'Dead reckoning: the church porch watch in British society', in H. E. Davidson, ed., *The Seer in Celtic and Other Traditions* (Edinburgh, 1989), pp. 80–99.

27. P. Griffiths, 'Secrecy and authority in late sixteenth- and early seventeenth-century London', *Hist. Jnl* 40 (1997), p. 929; W. Bray, ed., *The Diary of John Evelyn* (London, 1879), p. 4; Essex Record Office (hereafter ERO), Q/SR 109/19, 225/121, 300/29, 321/116, 329/140, 341/5, 344/95.

28. M. D. Harris, 'Laurence Saunders, citizen of Coventry', *English Hist. Rev.* 9 (1894), p. 645.

29. For almsgiving, see J. Boulton, 'Going on the parish: the parish pension and its meaning in the London suburbs, 1640–1724', in T. Hitchcock, P. King and P. Sharpe, eds, *Chronicling Poverty: The Voices and Strategies of the English Poor, 1640–1840* (London, 1997), pp. 32–3; S. Hindle, *On the Parish? The Micro-Politics of Poor Relief in Rural England, c. 1550–1750* (Oxford, 2004), pp. 148–9, 380–3.

appropriate forum for reminding them of their Christian duties. Such criticisms might be expressed in the seditious libels characteristic of the 'crime of anonymity', as they were at Wye (Kent), where a threatening letter censuring the hard-heartedness of clergy and gentry alike was cast into the porch during the dearth of 1630.[30] From this perspective, the symbolism of the shaming ritual in which, at Easter 1676, the Revd James Garth found the church porch of Hilperton (Wiltshire) filled with human excrement by the parishioners with whom he was in dispute would, doubtless, repay further investigation.[31]

The symbolism of Widow Greene's choice of refuge therefore vibrates across the centuries. The decoration and rebuilding of the church, for which the rich paid and from which the poor benefited, was a source of inter-parochial pride and emulation. The attachment between early modern parishioners and the parish church was, accordingly, highly emotional, conditioned by corporate senses of history and identity which may have been especially acute amongst the poor for whom the church was an unrivalled site of spiritual and material support. The porch in particular had enjoyed very significant liturgical and charitable functions which arguably remained rooted in popular consciousness long after the Reformation. Into the seventeenth century and beyond, therefore, the porch was a particularly significant arena in which notions of charity, solidarity and belonging might be negotiated.

Narratives of destitution

The following discussion investigates hard cases such as that of Widow Greene of Sprowston in the context of the tensions arising from the social construction of belonging in the English rural community at a time when the physical and moral boundaries of the parish were being reinforced by the introduction of formal welfare provision. As is well known, the Elizabethan poor laws of 1598 and 1601 enshrined the ancient scriptural distinction between the deserving and undeserving poor, requiring parish officers to relieve the known needy of the

---

30. TNA:PRO SP16/175/81; J. Walter, 'Public transcripts, popular agency and the politics of subsistence in early modern England', in M. Braddick and J. Walter, eds, *Negotiating Power in Early Modern Society: Order, Hierarchy and Subordination in Britain and Ireland* (Cambridge, 2001), pp. 142–3. For a later example from Scray (Kent) in 1768, see E. P. Thompson, 'The moral economy of the English crowd in the eighteenth century', *Past and Present* 50 (1971), p. 110. Cf. E. Thompson, 'The crime of anonymity', in D. Hay et al., *Albion's Fatal Tree: Crime and Society in Eighteenth-Century England* (London, 1975), pp. 255–308.
31. D. A. Spaeth, *The Church in An Age of Danger: Parsons and Parishioners, 1660–1740* (Cambridge, 2000), p. 14.

neighbourhood in their own homes and to expel wandering strangers back to the communities in which they had last worked.[32]

The criteria of belonging were, however, ambiguous and shifting. Who constituted the poor of the parish? Was settlement conferred by experience of those rituals of inclusion – baptism, marriage, perhaps even communion – through which the sense of place was socially constructed? Or was it rather a matter of social and economic participation, a function of residence, employment or apprenticeship for a specified period of time? And since the duties of kinship perforce extended to those family members who had migrated, perhaps temporarily, across the parish boundary, how did the legal obligations of the parish to its settled residents and the familial obligations of parents towards their children intersect? These were awkward questions in the seventeenth century and they remain awkward now, and not only in the historiographical context of a collection of essays designed to assess the extent to which English villages have been self-contained at various points in their history. After all, today's political debates about immigration policy, and especially about the role of putative entitlement to social security benefits in encouraging applications for asylum to the United Kingdom, turn on precisely the same issues: migrants represent both a reservoir of skilled and unskilled labour without which economic development might be hindered. At the same time they might be a potential drain on the resources of the welfare state.[33] Just as twenty-first-century Britain is struggling to resolve the paradox of international migration in the context of a welfare system predicated on notions of social insurance, seventeenth-century parishes wrestled with the dilemma of population turnover in a culture conditioned to believe that charity not only *began*, but also (as was argued with increasing regularity during the seventeenth century) *ended*, at home. From this perspective, the central place of the church porch in the mental maps of the destitute becomes clear, for this liminal space was of unrivalled strategic significance in securing access to the charity of the parish.

The causes of the destitution that led the migrant, and sometimes even the settled, poor to take refuge in church porches can occasionally be reconstructed in detail. Four case studies are particularly instructive of the acute tensions generated by the ambiguities of belonging during the early years of parish relief. In August 1634, for instance, two Warwickshire magistrates insisted that the overseers of the parish of Kineton provide a house for James Clarke, in order that he 'may thereby

---

32. 39 Elizabeth I, c. 3 (1598); 43 Elizabeth I, c. 2 (1601). For the context, see P. Slack, *Poverty and Policy in Tudor and Stuart England* (London, 1988), pp. 122–31; Hindle, *On the Parish?*, pp. 227–9.
33. D. Feldman, 'Migrants, immigrants and welfare from the old poor law to the welfare state', *Trans. Royal Hist. Soc.* 6th ser., 13 (2003), pp. 79–104.

be the better enabled to work and get his own livelihood'.[34] Habitation orders of this kind were extremely common in seventeenth-century England, and they were issued according to the logic of labour discipline. By providing targeted relief in kind in the form of house rent, magistrates argued, overseers could keep down relief costs, ensure that recipients did not misspend what was given them, and enforce the indigent to seek employment to support themselves. In this case, however, the parish officers of Kineton proved recalcitrant and refused to accept liability for Clarke, with the result that he, his wife and child were 'enforced to live in the church porch there to their great misery and danger of their lives' throughout the winter months. A further habitation order from the county bench in January 1635 seems, however, to have done the trick, and James Clarke was one of the three inhabitants of Kineton whose rents were paid by the overseers there into the late 1630s.[35]

John Salter and his pregnant wife Isabel were similarly successful in forcing the consciences of the parish officers at Sileby (Leicestershire) in 1637. Isabel had been dismissed from her job as a maidservant earlier that year, suspected of pilfering, and expecting a child which in fact turned out to be twins. Hastily married and forced to do public penance in Sileby church for fornication, the Salters sought accommodation in John's native parish of Seagrave, but were prevented from settling there. So they squatted in the church porch at Sileby until Isabel's former mistress brokered an agreement with the parish officers for two rooms rent-free in the town house.[36]

Others were not so fortunate, and in two cases, it seems, shivering nights in the church porch were the least of the troubles experienced by the destitute. In January 1655, Daniel Smith was removed from Bilton (Warwickshire) to Frankton, just over 4 miles away, where the parish officers were required to provide him, his wife and child with accommodation. The following Easter, however, it was reported that the overseers of Frankton had refused to cooperate with the result that Smith's wife 'for want of lodging and maintenance was almost starved and thereby forced to beg at Draycote where she was whipped and sent back to Bilton'. Although the justices fired off a second habitation order to the parish officers of Frankton, the inhabitants persuaded them to launch a further investigation of Smith's right of settlement. By October of 1655, it had been agreed that Smith was 'no poor of either parish', and was therefore 'to provide himself with a house where he can for his rent'. The consequences of this decision became apparent in

---

34. Ratcliff et al., eds, *Warwick County Records*, Vol. I, pp. 190–1.
35. Ibid.; Shakespeare Birthplace Trust Record Office, DR37/85/6/22.
36. Capp, 'Life, love and litigation', p. 69. For the Salters' subsequent fate, involving *inter alia* pilfering, suspected infanticide, indictment for felony and benefit of clergy, see Ibid., pp. 69–71.

January of 1656, when the magistrates were informed that 'by being driven up and down wanting an habitation', Smith was 'brought to extreme poverty'. He, his wife and child, had been 'violently cast out of part of an house where they were entertained at Frankton and were enforced to lie in the church porch, the woman being great with child and ready to be brought a bed'. Given her condition, the inhabitants were all the more determined to evict them even from this temporary shelter, with the result, Smith pleaded, that 'they must needs suddenly either perish through cold or become vagrants and beggars'. Smith's complaint, as we shall see, was likely to strike a chord with the magistrates, who were regularly reminded by the judiciary that no man, least of all a poor man, should be compelled to turn vagrant. The justices accordingly agreed a temporary settlement, requiring the parish officers of Frankton to house the Smiths and to give them 6d. weekly, but only until 'the wife be delivered and be able to go about in regard of their necessity'. Although this relief order implied that Smith's wife should either beg or seek casual labour after the birth of her child, the Frankton overseers were still dissatisfied. They succeeded in persuading the bench to order a further investigation by the local justice of the peace Sir Simon Archer, but were frustrated in their desire for a compromise on the immediate provision of relief. The Smiths subsequently disappear from the archive of the Warwickshire magistracy, and the poor survival of parish papers in the county prevents us from knowing for how long they had received relief in Frankton, if indeed they ever did so. The case is nonetheless highly revealing of the limited range of human sympathy at play in the politics of settlement.[37]

The case of Sarah Woodfall of Napton-on-the-Hill (Warwickshire) was even more problematic. Although she had lived there since 1635, she first came to the attention of the county bench in October 1650, when it was reported that she was in 'great misery and want', deserted by her husband and enforced with her five small children 'to lie in the church porch for want of an habitation'. The overseers were ordered to house her, but had failed to do so by January 1651 to her 'great prejudice and extreme suffering in this winter season'. By October 1651, her circumstances had deteriorated: she had another child and her husband was imprisoned for debt. The bench accordingly insisted that the parish officers provide her with a pension of 2s. od. a week, although whether they were already paying her rent is unclear. Either way, the ratepayers of Napton were enraged by the justices' generosity. 'She hath no need to be relieved in such sort as by her is pretended', they insisted: 'she misspends that which is given to her and is a woman most malicious against honest people'.[38] Although they were 'willing to

---

37. Ratcliff et al., eds, *Warwick County Records*, Vol. III, pp. 206, 226, 234, 245, 261.
38. For further evidence of ratepayers employing a behavioural calculus to reduce the generosity of transfer payments see Hindle, *On the Parish?*, pp. 379–98.

give allowance to her towards her maintenance what she shall necessarily want',
they succeeded in replacing the existing pension arrangement with a far more
vague stipulation that she should be allowed only 'what is necessary for one of her
condition, she behaving herself temperately'. This was not the end of the matter,
however, for she complained in the summer of 1653 that she was 'no wise able to
maintain herself' and was still destitute. The resulting arrangements, a habitation
order and a pension of 1s. od. a week, appear to have afforded her some measure
of security, but only until January 1660, when she complained that her landlord
had evicted her despite the fact that the village was paying part of her rent.[39]

These four case studies suggest that questions of settlement and belonging
ultimately turned on the discretion of parish officers who seem perfectly prepared
to evict and expel those poor migrants whose presence threatened to prejudice the
interests of the ratepayers. In doing so, however, they incurred the wrath of county
magistrates and assize judges, both of whom were concerned to prevent overseers
from deliberately exacerbating the vagrancy problem. This fundamental
disagreement between the officers of the county and those of the parish over the
nature and extent of overseers' obligations to relieve destitution turned on two
fundamental tensions generated by conflicting strands in late Elizabethan social
policy.

In the first instance, the poor relief statutes of 1598 and 1601 equated
'deservingness' with residence and settlement; and 'undeservingness' with
mobility and vagrancy. This distinction is reflected in the finely graded archival
residue of the legislation. Overseers' account books are replete with references to
the relief of the impotent 'poor of the parish', long-standing residents of the local
community who had lived respectable lives of labour until failing eyesight and
arthritic fingers had exhausted their capacity to support themselves. Constables'
account books, by contrast, include lists of gratuities paid to (and, less frequently,
expenses for the public whipping of) the idle wandering poor in an effort to
induce them to cross the parish boundary and trouble the ratepayers no more.[40]

From this perspective, those who drafted the poor laws might not
unreasonably be accused of assuming that English villages really were self-
contained, their obligations to their long-settled residents being compromised
only by the short-term pressure of long-distance migration at a time when,

---

39. Ratcliff et al., eds, *Warwick County Records*, Vol. III, pp. 38, 53, 76, 124–5, 183; Vol. IV, p. 78.
40. For conveniently printed collections of these differing sets of accounts, see S. Hindle, *The Birthpangs of Welfare: Poor Relief and Parish Governance in Seventeenth-Century Warwickshire* (Dugdale Soc. Occasional Papers, 40, 2000), pp. 37–74 (appendix II); M. Bennett, ed., *A Nottinghamshire Village in War and Peace: The Accounts of the Constables of Upton 1640–1666* (Thoroton Soc. Rec. Ser., 39, 1995).

according to the popular stereotype, desperate hordes of shiftless vagrants were tramping their way across the countryside in search of opportunities to gull the charitable and steal their goods. As students of vagrancy have shown, however, the popular terror of the tramp was a literary construction, created in the cheap print of the day.[41] The reality of geographical mobility in early modern England was altogether different, with population turnover far more convincingly characterised as the 'betterment migration' encouraged by developing markets for labour and marriage than as the 'subsistence migration' generated by the intersecting crises of warfare, dearth and industrial depression.[42] It is now as clear to historians as it was to contemporaries, therefore, that not all migrants, and not even all poor migrants, were vagrant.[43]

Judgements about the potential indigence of recent, perhaps even of long-standing, migrants to the parish must have been extraordinarily difficult to make, especially since the demand for the charity of neighbours and of the parish alike was so closely related to changing levels of need at different stages of the life cycle.[44] Did a newly arrived couple have the means to support themselves, let alone their real or potential offspring? Was the young woman already pregnant, and if so was there a husband, or failing that a putative father, who might be compelled to support her? Was the father of four likely to secure sufficiently regular employment to ensure that his children did not fall upon the parish? Were there alternative means of support available to the widow who had first come to the parish as a servant but was now too old or ill to support herself though her earnings? These were hard questions, and their answers were problematic for both parish officers and for the poor themselves. The implications of the fact that poverty was not only an enduring, perhaps even an inherited, condition, but also a function of universal human processes of ageing and childrearing, were therefore profound, especially in a welfare system designed to relieve 'the poor of the parish'.

In the second place, these difficulties over the nature of migration were compounded by tensions over the responsibility to find housing even for the

---

41.   Beier, *Masterless Men*, pp. 7–8; W. C. Carroll, *Fat King, Lean Beggar, Representations of Poverty in the Age of Shakespeare* (Ithaca, NY, 1996), pp. 70–96; C. Dionne and S. Mentz, eds, *Rogues and Early Modern English Culture* (Ann Arbor, 2004).

42.   P. Clark, 'Migration in England during the late seventeenth and early eighteenth centuries', reprinted in P. Clark and D. Souden, eds, *Migration and Society in Early Modern England* (London, 1987), p. 215.

43.   J. R. Kent, 'Population mobility and alms: poor migrants in the midlands during the early seventeenth century', *Local Population Studies* 27 (1981), pp. 35–51.

44.   T. Wales, 'Poverty, poor relief and the life-cycle: some evidence from seventeenth-century Norfolk', in R. M. Smith, ed., *Land, Kinship and Life-Cycle* (Cambridge, 1984), pp. 351–404.

settled poor. On the one hand, the 1589 statute on the taking of inmates and the building of cottages was designed to prevent the assimilation of poor strangers within parish communities, empowering magistrates to fine those householders or landlords who accommodated migrants without the permission of the parish officers; and requiring all others to guarantee to indemnify the parish of any relief expenditure incurred by the new residents.[45] On the other, the 1598 statute on relief of the poor required parish officers, with the consent of local landlords and at the charge of the ratepayers, to find accommodation for the impotent poor either by building 'convenyent Howses of dwelling' on those manorial wastes and commons which fell within the parish or by placing 'inmates or more families than one in one cottage or howse'.[46] The cumulative impact of the statutes was, therefore, ambiguous: parish officers were only obliged to house the destitute if they were settled, but the destitute could only gain settlement on terms which indemnified the parish from ever having to support them. This situation would have been relatively unproblematic in an environment characterised by very low levels of migration, but in a society in which population turnover between neighbouring communities was a significant structural feature, very many indigent people would find themselves destitute without settlement. These individuals were the most vulnerable to finding themselves squatting in the church porch.

The introduction of parish relief therefore posed a profound challenge to traditional notions of neighbourliness, solidarity and belonging. If ratepayers were legally obliged to contribute to the communal relief fund, they had a vested interest in ensuring that its assets would be distributed only to those genuinely impotent inhabitants whom they recognised as their own. The definition and identification of 'the poor of the parish' was, however, problematic, and the views of the judiciary on the one hand, and of parish officers and magistrates on the other, to say nothing of the destitute themselves, were often in conflict.

Interpretations of settlement

Until 1662, the only statutes that stipulated minimum periods of residence for a migrant to secure settlement, and by implication eligibility for poor relief, were

---

45. 31 Elizabeth I, c. 7 (1589), sect. vi. For its operation, see S. Hindle, 'Exclusion crises: poverty, migration and parochial responsibility in English rural communities, c. 1560–1660', *Rural Hist.* 7 (1996), pp. 125–49.
46. 39 Elizabeth I, c. 3 (1598), sect. v; J. Broad, 'Housing the rural poor in England, 1650–1850', *Ag. Hist. Rev.* 48 (2000), pp. 156–7, notes that this clause was significantly expanded in 1601: 43 Elizabeth c. 2, sects. iv and v.

those against vagrancy. In principle, the objective of all sixteenth-century vagrancy legislation was *invariably* to resettle vagrants in the parish of their birth. There were, nonetheless, various statutory experiments with the aim of identifying the parishes to which they should be sent should it prove impossible to discover their birthplace. Under the act of 1504, for instance, vagrants were to be removed either to their place of birth or 'to the place where they last made their abode above the space of three years'.[47] The act of 1547, however short-lived, marked an important departure in principle by mentioning only settlement by birth, a feature that almost certainly exacerbated the contemporary sense that it was unenforceable.[48] Although the relatively lenient (and more practical from the constable's point of view) alternative of settlement in the last parish of three years' residence was restored in 1572, it was further reduced in the parish officers' favour to one year in 1598.[49] Over the course of the seventeenth century, the minimum period required to achieve a settlement shrank even further, ultimately to forty days.[50] Even so, the most significant feature of sixteenth-century statutory definitions of settlement is their lack of applicability to the circumstances of most poor migrants, who were not, after all, vagrants.

When compulsory poor rates were finally stipulated in the legislation of 1598, the absence of any definition of settlement for anybody other than vagrants was sufficiently conspicuous to attract the attention of county magistrates almost immediately. This was particularly troubling since the 1598 statute was designed to *replace* rather than to *supplement* the act of 1572. As early as April 1598, the Essex bench indicated their understanding that the 1598 statute implied that 'no persons (other than Roages or Vagabonds) shalbe removed from their presente habitacions', but resolved to consult the judiciary about whether such expulsions, especially those of single mothers and children under the age of seven, might still be justified by the earlier legislation of 1572, which had empowered them to remove residents of less than three years' standing.[51] The West Riding justices were similarly perplexed, for their orders for relief of the poor drawn up at

47. 19 Henry VII, c. 12 (1504).
48. 1 Edward VI, c. 3 (1547). For the context, see C. S. L. Davies, 'Slavery and Protector Somerset: the Vagrancy Act of 1547', *Econ. Hist. Rev.*, 2nd ser. 19 (1966), pp. 533–49. The 1547 act was repealed by 3 and 4 Edward VI, c. 16 (1550).
49. 18 Elizabeth I, c. 5 (1572), sect. xvi. For the context, see P. Roberts, 'Elizabethan players and minstrels and the legislation of 1572 against retainers and vagabonds', in A. Fletcher and P. Roberts, eds, *Religion, Culture and Society in Early Modern Britain: Essays in Honour of Patrick Collinson* (Cambridge, 1994), pp. 29–55. Cf. 39 Elizabeth I, c. 3 (1598).
50. P. Styles, 'The evolution of the laws of settlement', *University of Birmingham Hist. Jnl* 9 (1963), reprinted in Styles, *Studies in Seventeenth-Century West Midlands History* (Kineton, 1978), pp. 175–204.
51. Tawney and Power, eds, *Tudor Economic Documents*, Vol. II, p. 363.

Knaresborough in June 1598 noted the need for 'better consideration' of the recent statute, which had already provoked widespread campaigns of exclusion in parishes now required by law to support the impotent. In the meantime, they had vainly sought to enforce the settlement provisions of the 1572 legislation: nobody was to be removed 'so longe as they contynue within the p[ar]ishe where they are now or have been inhabiting by the space of three yeares'. Parish officers had nonetheless taken advantage of the ambiguous status of the 1572 act to arbitrarily remove numerous long-settled residents for whose maintenance they did not wish to provide. The justices noted that those poor people who had been mistakenly (and illegally) expelled, some of who had 'bene inhabitinge & dwellinge in those places and townes from whence they are sent by the space of twentie yeares, some more, some lesse', were not 'Rooges nor wanderinge beggars within the meaning of the Statute, but ought to be relieved as the poore of the p[ar]ishe wher they so inhabited and wher they wrought when they were able to work'.[52] Almost immediately, therefore, the 1598 statute had provoked the shunting of the indigent, some of whom had been settled for a generation or more, back and forth across parish boundaries.

When the judges did offer an interpretation of the 1598 statute, they refused to confront the issue of what actually constituted a settlement, confining their comments to a reiteration of the twin principles that only the vagrant should be removed and only the impotent should be relieved.[53] This reading became the standard one, not least because it was widely publicised in magistrates' handbooks from William Lambarde's *Eirenarcha* of 1599 through the numerous editions of Michael Dalton's *Country Justice* into the eighteenth century.[54] Chief Justice Popham's 'resolucions' of 1607 effectively agreed with the article reprinted in *Eirenarcha*, that is: 'none ought to be sente to the places of their birthe or habitations but such onlie as are vagrante or wanderinge and not any that hath any dwelling in any parishe or be settled with their parents or any other in the parishe'.[55] This negative (or 'residual') definition of settlement was a mantra repeated by judges throughout the early seventeenth century, by Justice Sir James Whitelocke in Hereford in 1622; by Justice Francis Harvey in Cambridge in 1629; and by Chief Justice Sir Robert Heath on the Norfolk Circuit in 1633: the settled, these authorities all agreed, were all those who were not vagrant. For the first half of the seventeenth century at least, therefore, the prevailing judicial interpretation

52. J. Lister, ed., *West Riding Sessions Records, 1597–1642*, 2 vols (Yorks. Arch. Soc. Rec. Ser. 3, 54, 1888–1915), Vol. I, pp. 85–6 (orders 4, 5 and 6).
53. Bodleian Library, Oxford, MS Tanner, 91, fo. 163^v.
54. W. Lambarde, *Eirenarcha* (London, 1599), pp. 206ff (here quoting resolution no. 9); M. Dalton, *The Country Justice* (London, numerous edns, 1618–1727).
55. HMC, *Report on the Manuscripts of the Marquess of Lothian Preserved at Blickling* (London, 1905), p. 76.

of the relationship between settlement and eligibility for relief was that no one must be *compelled* to turn vagrant: although settlement itself went undefined, neither magistrates nor parish officers were legally entitled to remove the poor from any parish simply on the grounds of their destitution, still less if they were merely 'likely to become chargeable'.

By the 1650s, however, the tide was turning against the destitute, and Cromwell's law reformer William Sheppard seems to have been particularly influential in creating a body of case law which undermined the residential security of the indigent.[56] In 1656, he interpreted the 1629 Cambridge decision differently, arguing that Sergeant Harvey's reading had turned only on magistrates' *summary* powers: justices were, Sheppard insisted, empowered to deal with issues of settlement at quarter sessions, but not out-of-sessions where their competence extended only to rogues.[57] Sheppard also redefined the significance of the 1622 Hereford decision in which Whitelocke had ruled against a magistrate's habitation order on the grounds that although the destitute person was settled, he was not impotent. For Sheppard, this implied that 'none but the poor and impotent are thus to be ordered and settled': those likely to become chargeable, therefore might legally be removed.[58]

The notorious clauses of the 1662 settlement laws which empowered parish officers to remove pre-emptively any indigent person likely to become chargeable, amounted, therefore, not to a continuation of the advice of the judges but to a codification of the practices which had become increasingly prevalent in parishes by the 1640s and 1650s. Parliamentary critics had foreseen as early as 1598 that settlement might be denied not only to those that 'alreadye are ... poore', but also to those 'that maye be poore'. In 1661, Henry Townshend noted that the removal of 'those likely to be chargeable' was the 'generall present practice' in Worcestershire, and could trace precedents back to at least 1649.[59] Nor was

---

56. For Sheppard, see N. L. Matthews, *William Sheppard: Cromwell's Law Reformer* (Cambridge, 1984).

57. W. Sheppard, *The Whole Office of the Country Justice of Peace*, 3rd edn (London, 1656), p. 115.

58. The 1622 case turned on a dispute between the Herefordshire parishes of Laysters and Kimbolton, in which the JPs held the parish officers of Kimbolton in contempt for ignoring magistrates' instructions to provide a house for one Winde and his family. Whitelocke ruled that the Herefordshire bench had itself acted unlawfully because 'Winde was not a poor or impotent person within 43 Eliz 2 and the justices had no power by that law to compel and to provide a house for him, for he might provide one himself': W. Sheppard, *A Sure Guide for His Majesties Justice of Peace*, 2nd edn (London, 1669), p. 223. Dalton, *The Country Justice* (1682 edn), pp. 57–8 provides a summary of the case, which is more fully reported in *The Reports of Edward Bulstrode of the Inner Temple, Esquire*, 2nd edn (London, 1688), pt. I, pp. 347–8.

59. A. Hassell Smith, G. M. Baker, V. Morgan, J. Key, and B. Taylor, eds, *The Papers of Nathaniel Bacon of Stiffkey*, 4 vols (Norf. Rec. Soc., 46, 49, 53, 64, 1978–2000), Vol. IV, p. 35; R. D. Hunt, ed., 'Henry Townshend's "Notes of the Office of a Justice of the Peace"', *Worcs. Hist. Soc.: Miscellany II* (Leeds, 1967), pp. 106, 108.

Dalton's editor blind to the implications of this trend, criticising in 1682 the discretion implied by the words 'likely to be chargeable' as 'prejudicial to the commonwealth' on five grounds: that it unreasonably empowered excessive 'inspection and determination of another man's livelihood and condition'; that it might even on a remote possibility deprive a man of 'the company of friends and relations, choice of air and place of trade'; that it discouraged ingenuity and industry; that it restricted labour mobility; and encouraged depopulation, the 'greatest inconvenience an island can undergo'.[60] Although it is couched less in the idiom of Christian charity than of political economy, this is a remarkably liberal defence of the rights of the migrant poor against the powers of investigation and surveillance claimed by the parish authorities

To turn from the wainscot and sable of the court of King's Bench to the hovels and rags of the rural community, there can be little question that parish officers and ratepayers alike were alarmed by the likely impact of unchecked immigration on the level of poor relief expenditure. As early as 1569, the inhabitants of Stambourne (Essex) complained that a non-resident landlord of half a dozen cottages had not only accommodated 'such men theyr wyves and children as cannot els where have any dwellynge but are shifted from other townes and places' at the point where they were about to be a charge on the rates, but also racked the rents so that they 'are brought to playne beggary' in a village already overburdened with poor. The overseers of Emborough (Somerset) protested in 1619 that 'sundry strangers from remote parts' had lodged in the house of James and Margaret Haiball, a traffic which had led in turn to the births of numerous legitimate and illegitimate children who had fallen to the charge of the parish. As late as 1737, the parish officers of Troutbeck (Westmorland) complained that the subdivision of tenements tended 'to fill the town with poor and with ill members to the impoverishment and vexation' of the ratepayers; and that the erection of cottages brought 'a great charge of poor on the tenants and inhabitants' by 'settling children and servants'.[61] Complaints that greedy landlords let houses 'only to poor men which is like to breed a great charge to the inhabitants' were, it seems, ubiquitous in seventeenth-century England.[62]

Neither the destruction of cottages nor the eviction of inmates were, however, straightforward. The inability or reluctance of parish officers to provide sufficient housing stock meant that there was, quite simply, nowhere for poor migrants to

---

60. Dalton, *Country Justice* (1682 edn), p. 161.
61. ERO, Q/SR28/1; E. H. Bates-Harbin, ed., *Quarter Sessions Records for the County of Somerset*, 4 vols (Som. Rec. Soc., 23, 24, 28, 34, 1907–19), Vol. I, p. 254; M. A. Parsons, 'Poor relief in Troutbeck, 1640–1836', *Trans. Westmorland and Cumberland Antiquarian and Arch. Soc.*, 95 (1995), p. 172.
62. Bates-Harbin, ed., *Quarter Sessions Records for the County of Somerset*, Vol. I, p. 135.

go if they were evicted. The judges of the Norfolk Circuit were confronted with the realities of the situation at the Bury assizes in March 1634. They were well aware of 'the great increase of cottagers and inmates' and knew that under the terms of the 1589 statute 'the cottages ought to be pulled down'. The Suffolk bench nonetheless informed them that 'if the extremity of the law be used against them, these poor people would be exposed to misery and become a burthen to the parishes where they are settled'. Although Lord Chief Baron of the Exchequer Sir John Walter accordingly ordered that any cottages recently erected without licence were to be prevented, the parish officers having power to 'disturb & hinder the building and finishing thereof and destroy the same before any inhabitants be placed therein', he was nonetheless forced to concede that some cottages just had to be tolerated. He ordered a survey of 'what cottages and inmates there are in every parish, who are the inhabitants and who the reputed owners, and how long the cottages have been erected'. The judges and magistrates might then retrospectively license those cottages that were 'agreeable to the country'.[63]

This was, in fact, the context which generated the report of the Norfolk justices which recorded for posterity the case of Widow Greene of Sprowston with which this essay began.[64] The other cases to which the Norfolk magistrates drew attention expose the extraordinary fragility of domestic arrangements among the indigent, and in each they suggested that the judiciary should turn a blind eye, tolerating cottages and inmates their illegality notwithstanding. In Hainford alone, they identified John Barwell, 'an exceeding poore man with a wife & children', dwelling in a cottage 'built by himself some thirty yeares since'; Widow Mutton, 'a very poor woman' dwelling in an unlawful cottage sold to her by William Hinckes; Henry Wright and 'twoe very poore widdowes' cohabiting in a cottage who would 'have no place of aboade if they are turned away'; and John Sparke a cottager with an inmate 'both wch are very poore men'. In Felthorpe, they noted Robert Martyns, 'a very poore man that hath two very poore widows as inmates that pay a very small rent & cannot have better provision for them in the said town'; and Thomas Smith, who had erected a cottage but 'is now upon execution for debt and his wife with seven children inhabits the same'. In Beeston, finally, were John Randes, cottager, 'an old man & very poor', and Christopher Cook, 'a very poor man' with 'great charge of children', who had built a cottage with the help of the parish '& if he be put out he must lie in the street'. By tolerating cottages and inmates like these, and hundred of others like them across the parishes of Norfolk, county magistrates were effectively forcing parish officers to dispense a surrogate form of poor relief.

63. British Library, MS Additional, 39245, fo. 5 (reverse foliation).
64. TNA:PRO, SP16/272/44. See pp. 48–9 above.

There was an increasing recognition, therefore, that to pull down cottages and expel inmates was, after all, to turn the marginal poor to vagrancy. In some circumstances, the justices were actually encouraging householders to take lodgers for whom shelter could not otherwise be found. 'Most parishes,' wrote the justices of the peace of south-eastern Norfolk in 1636, are so 'fraighted with poore people destitute of habitations, as the number of cottages will not conteine them', and 'we are enforced not onely to admit of them, but even to presse divers others to receive som inmates, whoe were otherwise altogether unwilling'.[65] A more imaginative policy on cottages was adopted by the Worcestershire grand jury in 1663. Although they recognised that the lack of regulation of cottage building had caused the county 'to abound with poor more than any county in England that we know of', they nonetheless pleaded with the bench to suspend the prosecution of those who had erected them. Since the indiscriminate suppression of cottages would simply flood the countryside with vagrants, far better for the clergymen, officers and chief inhabitants of each parish to list all the cottages and indicate 'what persons they desire the cottages may be continued for'. The grand jury even argued that those cottagers who were to be tolerated should be allowed to live rent-free for life, presumably in an attempt to insulate the ratepayers from their demands for parish relief. The advantage for the overseers was that they should, on the death of the current tenants, be permitted either to pull the cottages down or to absorb them into the parish housing stock, thereby augmenting those resources which might be used to defray poor rates.[66]

In the light of all this scrutiny of the likelihood that they might become chargeable and of the evictions that often followed, it is unsurprising that the destitute should so frequently claim that they really had been forced to turn vagrant. This is a prominent theme in the petitions sent to the Somerset bench in the second and third decades of the seventeenth century. Agnes Powe claimed in 1614 that although she was born and had ever lived at Worle 'the parishioners will not suffer her there to abide'. Nicholas Webb alleged in 1615 that although he and his wife had lodged with his mother-in-law in Woolverton for four years, the lord of the manor had ordered their eviction. John Mountyer complained in 1619 that, despite two years residence as a married man in Milton Clevedon, the 'inhabitants there now go about to put him out of his house'. Margery Sybley a native of Isle Brewers complained in 1621 that she had recently been evicted from a house provided for her at parish expense for the last seven years, 'whereby she is utterly destitute'.[67] In 1617, the Somerset justices themselves crystallised the issue when

65. TNA:PRO, SP16/329/10.
66. HMC, *Reports on the Manuscripts in Various Collections*, Vol. I (London, 1901), pp. 323–4.
67. Bates-Harbin, ed., *Quarter Sessions Records for the County of Somerset*, Vol. I, pp. 105, 122, 262, 302.

investigating whether Hugh Kerle and his wife had become vagrant 'after he was put from' the parish of Pawlett or whether '*by the means of the parishioners* there he became as a rogue and vagrant': was Kerle a vagrant as a consequence of his own idleness or had he been forced into vagrancy by hostile ratepayers?[68]

The provision of housing for the poor, and especially for poor migrants, therefore tested the thresholds of tolerance of the communities in which they sought to settle. The questions of which poor migrants might be 'agreeable' to the country, and which cottages might be 'continued', were highly controversial. Some indication of how they might be answered is evident in an intriguing petition from the parishioners of Chewton to the Somerset bench in 1608. A sixty-year-old lead-miner named Richard Feare had been born in Great Chew and after many years working in the Mendip ore-fields had 'become almost blind and was likely to become chargeable to the parishioners of Chewton except speedy redress be had therein'. While he was working, Feare was welcome, offering skills and services for which there was demand in the parish. But failing eyesight and rheumatic limbs rendered his accommodation a far less attractive proposition. The parishioners pleaded that he ought to be relieved in the parish of his birth because 'he had never any settled abiding place in any sort with us at Chewton nor was ever taken as a parishioner there by receiving the Communion or performing any other duty belonging to a subject'. The definition of settlement offered by the parish officers of Chewton therefore augmented a simple residence requirement not only with an indication of social worth (the performance of 'duty', presumably in holding office or paying rates) but also with a symbol of belonging (being in charity with his neighbours by taking communion). The magistrates initially agreed, noting that because Feare had 'only lodged in a grove house during such time as he wrought' in the parish of Chewton, he was to be sent back to Great Chew. When they were informed that Feare had not been living in the parish of his birth 'this twenty and odd years', however, they changed their tune, and required the overseers of Chewton to relieve him.[69] As early as 1608, poor labouring men like Richard Feare were being shuttled back and forth across parish boundaries as ratepayers debated the geographical extent of their charitable obligations. Little surprise then that by 1635 Dalton could argue that 'for want of charity', poor people were 'much sent and tossed up and down from towne to towne and from countrey to countrey'.[70]

---

68. Ibid., Vol. I, pp. 197–8 (emphasis added).
69. Ibid., Vol. I, pp. 4–5, 11, 13.
70. Dalton, *Country Justice* (1635 edn), p. 99.

Thresholds of belonging

English villages had never, of course, been entirely self-contained. Medieval communities had long been permeable to external influences, integrated into the wider networks of the church, the state and the market.[71] (See in this volume pp. 22–7.) They had also, moreover, been characterised by a high degree of population turnover, the resulting pattern of kin dispersal ensuring that for all its flexibility and permissiveness, the early modern kinship system, like its medieval predecessor, was relatively 'loose', 'flexible' and 'permissive', and kin recognition was both 'narrow and shallow'.[72] Yet the Elizabethan poor laws by definition reinforced the boundaries of the local community by requiring that each parish should look after its own: after 1598, parishes had to be well defended in order to prevent the unnecessary inflation of welfare costs. Until the adaptation of the settlement laws (originally passed in 1662) in the eighteenth century made it possible for a pensioner to reside in one parish and receive relief from another, his or her parish of 'settlement', the accommodation of poor migrants was a particularly sensitive issue, implying the policing of parish boundaries and the locking of church porches alike.[73]

From this perspective, the English village was peculiarly hostile to poor migrants in the years after 1598. Such hostility arguably diminished only when evolving poor-law practice created a framework in which a parish might accommodate a stranger without committing itself to relieve them should they become chargeable. Although non-resident relief was never explicitly recognised in law, examples of the practice can be cited from the late seventeenth century, as in Cambridge in 1690 or Alcester (Warwickshire) in 1693.[74] By the early eighteenth century, perhaps one in three of those relieved in the parishes of Lancashire or

71. R. M. Smith, ' "Modernization" and the corporate medieval village community in England: some sceptical reflections', in A. H. R. Baker and D. Gregory, eds, *Explorations in Historical Geography* (Cambridge, 1984), pp. 140–79.

72. D. Postles, 'Migration and mobility in a less mature economy: English internal migration, c. 1200–1350', *Social Hist.* 25 (2000), pp. 285–99; K. Wrightson and D. Levine, *Poverty and Piety in an English Village. Terling, 1525–1700*, 2nd edn (Oxford, 1995), pp. 187–97.

73. The best introduction to the settlement laws is K. D. M. Snell, 'Settlement, poor law and the rural historian: new approaches and opportunities', *Rural Hist.* 3 (1992), pp. 145–72. For studies of the implications of 'non-resident' or 'out-parish' relief, see, P. Sharpe, ' "The bowels of compation"': a labouring family and the law, c. 1790–1834'; J. S. Taylor, 'Voices in the crowd: the Kirkby Lonsdale township letters, 1809–36'; and T. Sokoll, 'Old age in poverty: the record of Essex pauper letters, 1780–1834', all in Hitchcock et al., eds, *Chronicling Poverty*, pp. 87–108, 109–26, 127–54.

74. E. M. Hampson, 'Settlement and removal in Cambridgeshire, 1662–1834', *Cambridge Hist. Jnl* 2 (1926–8), p. 287; Styles, 'The evolution of the laws of settlement', pp. 62–3. I am grateful to Keith Snell and Steve King for discussions of the origins and spread of non-resident relief.

Somerset were residing elsewhere, a tendency which surely undermined the imperative to remove those considered likely to become chargeable, and rendered the imperative to police the parish boundary less urgent. In the days before such 'non-resident' relief became common, however, overseers were required to police the parish boundaries in order to protect the interests not only of their fellow ratepayers but also of the resident poor whose collection might by diminished by the increased burden of 'poor strangers crept amongst them'.[75] Although it is not the purpose of this paper to argue that the English village was in general terms becoming *more* self-contained in late sixteenth and seventeenth century, the years between 1598 and the mid-eighteenth century arguably represent a period in which inhabitants and migrants alike were peculiarly sensitive to the physical and moral thresholds of belonging to the early modern community.

The local politics at play in accommodating the poor expose the degree of tolerance towards poor strangers which prevailed in the rural village. As early as 1598 the Norfolk MP Nathaniel Bacon had warned that one implication of the poor law reform then being debated in parliament was that 'the poore' would be 'greatlie disapoynted both of releif and habitacion'. The draft statute, he insisted, gave an incentive for landlords and parish officers to evict those migrants who 'maye be[come] poore'. Those considered likely to be chargeable would, he argued, 'be driven from all townes to lye in the highe wayes and feildes without habitacion'. Bacon was disgusted: 'the poore', he wrote, 'must be still amongst us, Christ said so'.[76] Despite this robust statement of the charitable imperative, the Elizabethan relief statutes by definition generated hostility to the homeless, even to those who were perceived to be at risk of becoming homeless, at least until the settlement laws created the possibility of non-resident relief. As the judges chased each other through the thickets of the law in trying to define settlement and vagrancy adequately during the first half of the seventeenth century, the poor complained that they were driven to lie under hedges, in barns, and in church porches.

There were, inevitably, those who tired of these debates, and, frustrated by the circularity of legal definitions of belonging, chose to close off even the last refuges of the destitute. As early as 1605, Archbishop Bancroft's visitation articles for the province of Canterbury were asking whether the

> Church wardens and Questmen, from time to time doe their dilligence, in not suffring any idle persons or loytererers, to abide either in the Church-yard or Church-porch in Seruice or Sermon time, but causing them either to come into the

---

75. For this idiom, see S. Hindle, 'Power, poor relief and social relations in Holland Fen, *c.* 1600–1800', *Hist. Jnl* 41 (1998), p. 91.
76. Smith et al., eds, *The Papers of Nathaniel Bacon*, Vol. IV, p. 35.

Church to heare Diuine seruice, or to depart, and not to disturbe such as are hearers there.[77]

By the 1660s, even the assize judges, who (as we have seen) were wedded to the principle that no man should be forced into vagrancy, argued that the obligation of parish officers to provide housing for the poor did not extend to 'lusty yong marryed people': Sir Robert Hyde insisted at the Worcestershire Assizes in 1661 that 'yf yong men marry together before they have howses ther is no law to enforce churchwardens and overseers by the Justices to find howses; but yf they cannot get any, let them lye under an oke'.[78] These attitudes were not, by this time, entirely uncharacteristic of the magistracy either. When taken to task by the Norfolk justice Robert Doughty for the fact that John Woods, his wife and a seven-week-old child were found sleeping rough at Ingworth in 1665, they retorted that Doughty's fellow justice of the peace Oliver Neave had told them to 'let him lie in the church porch'.[79]

Whether or not this statement was fictional, an example of special pleading on the part of delinquent parish officers, its lack of charity almost pales into insignificance alongside the hostility to the destitute expressed by one Caroline clergyman, to whom the last word on the thresholds of tolerance in the 'self-contained' village should be given. In 1639, Ithiel Smart the vicar of Wombourne (Staffordshire) committed an act of enclosure, hedging the migrant poor out of access to the circuits of charity and belonging in the local community: he had the church porch gated, railed and bolted in order that 'idle and impotent people might not lodge therein as [they had done] in former times'.[80]

77. Articles to be inquired of, in the first metropoliticall visitation, of the most reuerend father, Richarde by Gods prouidence, archbushop [sic] of Canterbury, and primat of all Englande in, and for the dioces of Noruuich, in the yeare of our Lorde God 1605, and in the first yeare of His Graces translation (London, 1605), sig. A4r.
78. Hunt, ed., 'Henry Townshend's "Notes"', p. 107.
79. Rosenheim, ed., Notebook of Robert Doughty, 61.
80. S. Shaw, The History and Antiquities of Staffordshire, 2 vols (London, 1798–1801), Vol. II, p. 217. In this respect Smart resembles Alexander Strange of Layston, another Caroline clergyman whose views on the migrant poor were, to say the least, exclusionary: S. Hindle, 'Introduction: the clergy and the politics of poor relief in a Hertfordshire parish', in H. Falvey and S. Hindle (eds), 'This Little Commonwealth': Layston Parish Memorandum Book, 1607–c.1650 & 1704–c.1747 (Hertfordshire Record Publications 19, Hertford 2003), pp. xi–xlvii. Cf. G. Winstanley, 'A new-year's gift for the parliament and army', in C. Hill, ed., Winstanley: The Law of Freedom and other Writings (Cambridge, 1983), p. 201: 'The law is but the strength life and marrow of the kingly power, upholding the conquest still, hedging some into the earth, hedging out others; giving the earth to some and denying the earth to others, which is contrary to the law of righteousness, who made the earth at first as free for one as for another. '

4

'Ancient inhabitants':
mobility, lineage and identity in English rural communities, 1600–1750

HENRY FRENCH

It is now over forty years since Peter Laslett's preliminary researches into population mobility uncovered the 'startling fact ... that a settled, rural, perfectly ordinary Stuart community could change its composition by well over half, getting on for two-thirds, in a dozen years'.[1]

As is shown in Table 4.1, subsequent studies have confirmed this 'startling fact' by demonstrating it repeatedly across the country, in a variety of settlements and time periods. In 1979, Peter Clark summarised the findings of the first generation of social historians about migration.[2] By then, it had become evident that among rural dwellers of both sexes 'nearly seven in ten' were mobile at some point during their lives. Most of these rural migrants were unmarried, and aged between twenty-one and thirty. Roughly half of all migrants travelled no more than 10 miles, with only 10 per cent travelling more than 40 miles. There were some regional differences, with the mobile proportion being lower (nearer 50 per cent) in western counties, and higher in eastern ones (nearer 70 per cent). There were also social differences, so that 'gentlemen and merchants, as well as professional men ... registered the greatest average distances travelled'.[3] In short, as Clark observed, it was clear that 'the great mass of English people, men and women, country-dwellers as well as townspeople, migrated at some time in their lives'.[4]

These findings were important because they cut across layers of assumptions in both academic and popular discourses in which village 'communities' down to the twentieth century had been idealised as authentic or organic centres of belonging, because their populations were geographically immobile and

1. P. Laslett, 'Clayworth and Cogenhoe', in P. Laslett, *Family Life and Illicit Love in Earlier Generations: Essays in Historical Sociology* (Cambridge, 1977), p. 66.
2. P. Clark, 'Migration in England during the late seventeenth and early eighteenth centuries', *Past and Present* 83 (1979), pp. 57–90. A more recent summary is provided in I. D. Whyte, *Migration and Society in Britain 1550–1830* (Basingstoke, 2000), pp. 22–62.
3. Clark, 'Migration', p. 81.
4. Ibid., p. 72.

Table 4.1 Percentage of population remaining after c. ten and twenty years in ten English parishes, 1618–1861

Parish	County	First date	Last date	Years	% Remaining	% Children
c. Twenty years						
Odiham	Hants.	1721	1740	19	56.0	–
Swinderby	Lincs.	1771	1791	20	76.6	25.7
Mean %					64.8	
Median %					61.8	
c. Ten years						
Clayworth	Notts.	1676	1688	12	61.8	36.7
Cogenhoe	N. Hants.	1618	1628	10	52.2	–
Long Melford	Suffolk	1676	1684	8	39.0	–
Highley	Shrops.	1696–8	1706–8	10	50.0	–
Binfield	Berks.	1790	1801	11	49.0	–
Bolton Abbey	Yorks.	1851	1861	10	50.5	16.1
Laxton	Notts.	1851	1861	10	50.6	25.0
Elmdon	Essex	1851	1861	10	46.3	26.8
Mean %					48.2	
Median %					50.0	

Sources: R. Tinley and D. Mills, 'Population turnover in an eighteenth-century Lincolnshire parish in comparative context', *Local Population Studies* 52 (1994), p. 36; G. Nair, *Highley: The Development of a Community 1550–1880* (Oxford, 1988), p. 149; B. Stapleton, 'Family strategies: patterns of inheritance in Odiham, Hampshire, 1525–1850', *Continuity and Change* 14 (1999), p. 387; L. Boothman, 'Mobility and stability in Long Melford, Suffolk in the late seventeenth century', *Local Population Studies* 62 (1999), p. 38; M. Escott, 'Residential mobility in a late eighteenth-century parish: Binfield, Berkshire 1779–1801', *Local Population Studies* 40 (1988), p. 23.

embedded in dense networks of kin. As Richard Smith noted, these assumptions had been implicit even in the late nineteenth century, in the founding debates about the legal and administrative history of manors and vills between Maine and Maitland, and the sociology of 'modernisation' conceived by Tönnies. Smith also observed how concepts of community and social change based upon these intellectual foundations continued to influence several subsequent generations of English social historians.[5] Similarly, Susan Wright has observed the same preconceptions at work among those pioneering British social anthropologists who undertook the first generation of 'community studies' between the 1930s and 1960s.[6] She characterised these as united by their focus upon remote rural settlements, which were seen to represent 'an 'unchanged' vestige of what was perceived as an 'earlier' existence, soon to be wiped out by the influence of distant urban centres'.[7]

5.   R. M. Smith, ' "Modernization" and the corporate medieval village community in England: some sceptical reflections', in A. R. H. Baker and D. Gregory, eds, *Explorations in Historical Geography: Interpretative Essays* (Cambridge, 1984), pp. 140–80.
6.   S. Wright, 'Image and analysis: new directions in community studies', in B. Short, ed., *The English Rural Community: Image and Analysis* (Cambridge, 1992), pp. 195–217.
7.   Wright, 'New directions', p. 200.

Yet, if this unexpected rate of population turnover appeared at odds with the ideas of modern observers, it also seems at variance with the comments and assumptions of contemporaries in the early modern period. This dichotomy is revealed most fully in the case of the most detailed, intimate and vivid account of seventeenth-century village life, Richard Gough's *History of Myddle*. The long and complicated family histories related by Gough seem to provide concrete evidence of earlier, static conceptions of village life, where everyone knew everyone else, and knew everything about everyone else. However, as David Hey has shown, Myddle was not immune from the social consequences of Laslett's 'startling fact'. Nineteen of the ninety families living in the village in the later seventeenth century had a son or daughter away in London, while almost a half the marriage partners of Myddle-born inhabitants came from outside the village (although almost none came from outside the county).[8]

This chapter seeks to reconcile Gough's 'village in the mind', in which the history of the 'community' was conceived of as an assembly of the histories of the pew-owning families within it, with the bald demographic fact that nearly a half the marriage partners in that settlement during his lifetime were drawn from elsewhere in the county.[9] It takes Gough's *History* as an illustration of the significance accorded by contemporaries to length of residence, and of their emphasis upon 'ancient inhabitants' and families of long standing over the newcomers in their rural townships. Examining Gough's social values in more detail, it seeks to understand why he seems to have adopted this social perspective, and sets his views in the context of the opinions of other parish rulers, to assess their wider significance. It then attempts to reconcile the reality of a mobile rural populace with those social values that praised stability and dynastic longevity, by analysing the social differences in rates of population turnover in rural settlements. By identifying greater intra-generational stability among those of Gough's social standing, this chapter suggests that those who privileged personal roots and familial longevity may have been praising characteristics that they were the most able to maintain. For those lower down the social scale, 'belonging' may have been more a matter of personal acceptance rather than of ancestry.

8.   D. Hey, *An English Rural Community: Myddle under the Tudors and Stuarts* (Leicester, 1974), Table 10, p. 201.
9.   The phrase 'village in the mind' is taken from M. Strathern, 'The village as an idea: constructs of village-ness in Elmdon, Essex', in A. P. Cohen, ed., *Belonging: Identity and Social Organisation in British Rural Cultures* (Manchester, 1982), p. 249.

Family and inheritance at Myddle

As David Hey has remarked, 'Richard Gough's book is the most remarkable local history ever written ... a pungent commentary upon all, or nearly all, the fellow members of his rural community'.[10] In assessing the insights that it gives us into the 'self-contained village', we need first to consider the purpose behind this work. Gough appears to have intended his volume as one of reference, in which 'there is nothing herein mentioned which may not by chance att some time or other happen to bee needful to some person or other'.[11] Above all, it was directed at explaining the rights by which the parishioners held their pews in church. This was necessary because these pews were not apportioned according to wealth, or rateable value, but by property ownership and inheritance. This imperative required Gough to focus on 'the descent and pedigree of all, or most part of the families in this side of the parish', which he did, warts and all.[12] It meant that he accorded particular attention to 'antient' families, whose roots in the community, and rights in the church, were of long standing. These included families such as the Lloyds, who were 'very antient, if not the antientest family in this part of the parish, as appears by antient deeds'.[13] Gough acknowledged other elements of heredity, but regarded them less positively. The Tylers were also 'very antient in this parish', but were regarded by Gough as a source of 'bad blood', flowing through four generations from William Tyler, of whom Gough noted 'many had done wickedly, butt hee excelled them all'.[14]

Gough also seems to have regarded long lineage among incomers in positive terms. Although Richard Mather was 'a stranger in this country', he 'marryed a gentlewoman whose surname was Wollascott; shee was descended of that antient and worthy family of the Wollascotts of Wollascott, an antient farme neare Preston Gubballs'.[15] William Crosse was son of Adam Crosse 'of Yorton, of an antient and substantiall family there',[16] while Michael Baugh of Clive (Gough's great-uncle) 'was a person of antient family there'.[17] For Gough lineage was merely one among many components of reputation, to be assessed alongside personal (particularly moral) characteristics. It provided its possessor with an entry into the village community, by linking the individual to a known pedigree and a body of existing

---

10. R. Gough, *The History of Myddle*, ed. D. Hey (London, 1981), introduction, p. 7.
11. Gough, *Myddle*, p. 78.
12. Ibid.
13. Ibid., p. 95.
14. Ibid., p. 176.
15. Ibid., p. 126.
16. Ibid., p. 130.
17. Ibid., p. 162.

social knowledge. As the 'wickedness' of the Tylers indicates, such knowledge was not always synonymous with approbation. Similarly, descent from an 'antient, substantiall' family gave the individual a history to live up to, and a standard against which he or she could be measured – a comparison that was not always favourable. In the case of his great-uncle, Michael Baugh, Gough noted sadly that he was 'allwaies in a decaying condition', despite his ancestry, the absence of any obvious personal weaknesses, and the financial support of Gough's great-grandfather, grandfather and uncles. William Crosse's addiction to drunkenness also outweighed his family background and careful education. Lineage located the individual within the dynastic histories of the locality, but Gough rarely regarded it as the decisive element in determining his or her fate.

In exhibiting a certain, if qualified, bias in favour of the known over the unknown, Gough was merely expressing a preference that seems to have been prevalent among other village dwellers in the seventeenth century. Martin Ingram has demonstrated that in early seventeenth-century Wiltshire outsiders were three times more likely to be prosecuted for theft compared to other villagers, and that 90 per cent of those convicted in such cases came from the outside.[18] Steve Hindle has also emphasised that in distributing poor relief or allocating charitable or other communal resources prosperous ratepayers (such as Gough)[19] tended to discriminate in favour of the settled poor of long-standing, over recent arrivals and those who were rootless.[20] Again, the eight settlement cases that Gough appended to his History testify to this concern.[21] A number of other studies have also demonstrated how propertied villagers sought to exclude the economically marginal from access to commons, wastes and woods, in the face of population growth in the sixteenth, seventeenth and eighteenth centuries.[22] Beneath these

18. M. Ingram, 'Communities and courts: law and disorder in early seventeenth-century Wiltshire', in J. S. Cockburn, ed., Crime in England 1550–1800 (London, 1977), pp. 132–3. Gough illustrated this trend with his tale about John Aston, 'a sort of a silly fellow, very idle and much given to stealing of poultry and small things'. Although Aston was often caught, and beaten by his victims, he was only prosecuted when 'at last hee grew insufferable', but even then was convicted only of a misdemeanour rather than a felony, at the judge's direction: Gough, Myddle, pp. 145–6.

19. Gough noted that when his father married in 1633 he paid 4d. poor rates per annum, but that now in 1701 he himself was assessed at £1 per annum: Gough, Myddle, p. 146.

20. S. Hindle, 'A sense of place? Becoming and belonging in the rural parish, 1550–1650' in A. Shepard and P. Withington, eds, Communities in Early Modern England (Manchester, 2000), pp. 96–114; S. Hindle, On the Parish? The Micro-Politics of Poor Relief in Rural England c. 1550–1750 (Oxford, 2004), pp. 127, 147, 152, 322, 335, 347n, 410.

21. Gough, Myddle, pp. 251–64.

22. S. Birtles, 'Common land, poor relief and enclosure: the use of manorial resources in fulfilling parish obligation, 1601–1834', Past and Present 165 (1999), pp. 74–106; J. Broad, 'The smallholder and cottager after disafforestation: a legacy of poverty?', in J. Broad and R. Hoyle, eds, Bernwood: The Life and Afterlife of a Forest (Preston, 1997), pp. 90–107; R. W. Bushaway, 'From custom to crime: wood gathering in eighteenth- and early nineteenth-century England: a focus for conflict

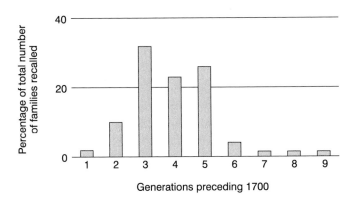

Figure 4.1 Percentage distributions of generations of families recalled by Richard Gough, Myddle, 1701 (N=70)

jurisdictional disputes and local solidarities lay the 'culture of local xenophobia' highlighted recently by Keith Snell, that spawned inter-parochial conflicts over everything from access to commons and settlement rights to fist fights and football matches.[23] In these respects, the social networks revealed in Gough's account had sharp legal and economic edges, as well functioning as the transmission mechanism for 'picturesque' gossip and innuendo.

The other significant feature of the *History of Myddle* is that *Richard Gough* wrote it, rather than any other inhabitant of the village. He could do so because he and his family were an unusual point of stability in the restless mobility of rural existence. As he demonstrated proudly in the *History*, not only had he lived most of his life in the village but also his family had been prosperous yeomen in Newton in Myddle township for five generations before Richard was born in 1634. As we have

22. Cont.

in Hampshire, Wiltshire and the south', in J. G. Rule, ed., *Outside the Law: Studies in Crime and Order, 1650–1810* (Exeter, 1982), pp. 65–101; S. Hindle, 'Power, poor relief and social relations in Holland Fen, *c.* 1600–1800', *Hist. Jnl* 41 (1998), pp. 67–96; P. King, 'Gleaners, farmers and the failure of legal sanctions in England, 1750–1850', *Past and Present* 125 (1989), pp. 116–50; J. M. Neeson, *Commoners: Common Right, Enclosure and Social Change in England 1700–1820* (Cambridge, 1993); L. Shaw-Taylor, 'Labourers, cows, common rights and parliamentary enclosure: the evidence of contemporary comment, *c.* 1760–1810', *Past and Present* 171 (2001), pp. 95–126; M. Turner and D. Woodward, 'Theft from the common man: the loss of "common" use rights in England', in T. Brotherstone and G. Pilling, eds, *History, Economic History and Marxism: Essays in Memory of Tom Kemp* (London, 1996), pp. 51–78.

23. K. D. M. Snell, 'The culture of local xenophobia', *Social Hist.* 28 (2003), pp. 1–30.

seen, in this respect, Gough was clearly the exception rather than the rule in Myddle, or anywhere else.[24]

If we examine the *History* in more detail, we can see that, in fact, this familial experience shapes it in two respects. From the perspective of 1700 (when he wrote it), Gough's account is focused on the historical middle distance, on events that determined entitlements in his own generation, and the two that preceded it. In producing his descents of the seating rights, he drew on two sources of memory – his own, and those of his parents and grandparents. Figure 4.1 illustrates how many generations Gough could recall before 1700. For roughly one-third of the pew rights he mentioned, he could recall three generations before 1700 (the current one, plus the parental and grandparental ones).[25] Given that he was, himself, sixty-six years old by then, this meant (effectively) that he could recall them in his childhood, or could place them personally within stories that he had learned in adulthood. In addition, he could recall information about pew rights over four generations in another sixteen instances, and five generations in a further eighteen cases. In all, among the forty-four families who enjoyed seating rights in Myddle church in 1700, Gough was able to mention a median of three generations of their predecessors. Therefore, he could supplement his own memories with those of his father, and his grandfather (who Gough seems to have known),[26] extending back to the generations born 1600–10 and 1570–80. Beyond that limit, Gough's knowledge of the sixth to ninth generations before 1700 was generally very sketchy, and relied increasingly on historical sources. The distinct immobility of the Goughs supplied Richard with his information, but the limits of personal and familial memory constrained what even he could recall.

It is also interesting to locate those he mentions within the wider family trees provided by David Hey. In general, possibly because his primary task was to describe the ownership of pews rather than general family histories, Gough tends to restrict his attention to the main heirs, supplemented only by those notable for

---

24. Ibid., pp. 152–70.
25. In this context, the term 'generation' is necessarily imprecise. Where Gough indicates that the pew right descended from parent to child it is easy to count this as the movement from one generation to the next. Where land or leases were sold, or property passed laterally between siblings or 'cousins', it has been regarded as occurring *within* an existing generation, unless Gough gives supplementary information to suggest that this marks an inter-generational transfer, or that it occurred over an extended period of time. It should also be noted that the term 'generation' refers to the assumption that a thirty-year time period had elapsed, rather than the occurrence of a specific inheritance *within* a particular family.
26. He records that his grandfather was 'a proper tall man', while his grandmother was 'a very litle woman', and that his grandfather 'was thicke of heareing for many yeares before hee dyed, and in his old age was taken with a palsy, and was lame some yeares', implying that he lived into Gough's youth: Ibid., pp. 168–9.

their deeds or misdeeds. He seems largely to have ignored those who died young, those unconnected with the descent of the pew right, and also (displaying more discretion than we might otherwise accord him) to minimise his mentions of the living. This is evident in his treatment of the Hordley family, for example, where his memory stretches back five or six generations, but is in other respects fairly selective.[27] He mentions John Hordley III, born in 1548, died in 1625, but does not recall the two preceding generations traced by Hey. Gough mentions John III's second wife Katherine Ashe, and his surviving son, Andrew, born 1586, died 1640, and his wife Joan Formston, who died in old age in 1677, well within Gough's remembrance. Andrew's children were Gough's exact contemporaries, and he records Thomas (born 1622), Andrew (born 1625), John V (born 1635) and Sarah (born 1637). Gough would have grown up alongside these four children, and they feature most extensively in his memories. Significantly, he mentions none of the children of John V (who were born c. 1664–74). This family history illustrates how Gough's recall was shaped by the central concern of his parish history, and the limits of his own and his family's memories. He was usually unable to relate anything about the generations that had died before 1560, and he devotes less attention to those born after 1660, unless they rendered themselves worthy of special comment. This illustrates that the chronological focus of his reminiscences was on the generation who were adult during his youth and early adulthood, and on his parents' and grandparents' memories of their immediate ancestors. For this 'ancient inhabitant' writing in 1700, the effective limit of memory extended back to the second half of the sixteenth century, even if the bulk of the recollections dwelt on the first half of the seventeenth century.

Residence in the parish

For Gough, clearly, the depth of a family's social roots was important in locating it in the church, in its relations to other families, and even in contributing to its personal and moral character – which formed such important additional components in Gough's estimation of families. In essence, Gough's literary purpose – recording the rights by which families occupied pews – ensured that he privileged descent, because descent was the basis of seating entitlement, and because it embodied precedent. In this way, Gough acted like those other 'ancient inhabitants' who were wheeled out in countless Chancery cases, as Adam Fox has noted, to employ their memories to establish custom.[28] In a legal system that depended on precedent, the elderly, and families of long standing, might acquire a

27. Ibid., p. 156.
28. A. Fox, *Oral and Literate Culture in England 1500–1700* (Oxford, 2000), pp. 275–9.

social significance out of all proportion to their financial worth (or the respect previously accorded to them in their lifetimes). As Richard Hoyle has also emphasised recently, although in principle 'custom' was supposed to establish matters beyond the memory of man (and the beginning of Common Law recording in 1189), in practice it tended to be a perspective on past practice that was similar in its chronological span to Richard Gough's memory.[29] Reviewing the rights claimed by customary tenants in the sixteenth century, Hoyle observes that such custom 'is frequently an account of their treatment in the generation before last. It is how the present manorial lord's father's or grandfather's officers conducted matters on the estates'.[30] As a result, their 'histories' of entitlements and rights tended to match the scope of Gough's History of the rights by which his neighbours held their seats in church.

The identity of most such 'ancient' witnesses was determined primarily by the accident of longevity. However, there is also evidence that contemporaries had certain preconceptions about the likely social profile of the 'ancient families' of the parish. The most obvious of these assumptions was that those who owned land, particularly those who owned manors, were likely to have been the longest settled members of the community, and (like Richard Gough) would be best able to contribute to the history of their settlement. This explains the research strategy of the early eighteenth-century antiquary William Holman, in undertaking his projected History of Essex (eventually completed by Philip Morant).[31] Holman's preferred method of reconstructing the history of each of the manors of Essex was to write to their owners and ask them to furnish deeds and evidence of their family history. He assumed that such landowning families would be of long standing, and that they would therefore be capable of supplying him with extensive manorial histories, or lengthy runs of deeds. In fact, he was frustrated repeatedly by the active land market and geographic (and social) mobility in the county. Essex, it seems, had few Richard Goughs.

For example, in June 1723 Robert Beverly of Fyfield apologised to Holman for his lack of cooperation, citing his ignorance of the history of his parish. This was due to his shallow roots there, or elsewhere in the county. 'As to the Pedigree of my

---

29. R. Hoyle, 'Redefining copyhold in the sixteenth century: the case of timber rights', in B. J. P. Van Bavel and P. Hoppenbrouwers, eds, Landholding and Land Transfer in the North Sea Area (late Middle Ages–Nineteenth Century) (Turnhout, 2004), pp. 250–64.
30. Hoyle, 'Redefining copyhold', p. 254.
31. For a more extensive consideration of Holman and his collaborators see H. R. French, '"Ingenious & Learned Gentlemen": social perceptions and self-fashioning among parish elites in Essex, 1680–1740', Social Hist. 25 (2000), pp. 56–63. For the genealogy of the project to write a history of Essex, see R. Sweet, Antiquaries. The Discovery of the Past in Eighteenth-Century Britain (London, 2004), p. 54.

Family, There is no occasion in the least to insert it into the antiquities of Essex, in which none of my Relations lived before me, nor have I any kin living to be hereafter inserted'.[32] Beverly was not alone among Holman's Essex correspondents in decrying his own status as a significant landowner, because of the shallowness of his roots in his community.[33] Even those descended from well-established parochial families, such as Joseph Mann, an attorney and vestryman in Braintree, were often little better equipped to help. Holman's research collaborator Samuel Dale had talked to Mann, 'but I found he knows little of his own Ancestors', and appeared to care even less.[34]

In other contexts (where the personal stakes were higher) the parochial rulers to whom Holman appealed for evidence could take a different attitude, but one that illustrates the operation of a similar social assumption, linking wealth, length of residence and social importance. Along with Joseph Mann, Samuel Dale was a member of the Braintree 'Select' Vestry, a 'company' of twenty-four self-selecting parishioners who ruled a cloth-producing town of some 2,000–3,000 (mostly poor) inhabitants. In 1713, the parish had been split by a dispute over membership of the vestry, in which the clique of vestrymen had been opposed by 'the forty-eight', intent on opening up this meeting to all interested ratepayers. The issue of access to the vestry came to a head over the election of Peter Peers, a wealthy clothier, whose supporters described him as 'very well knowne to be one of the most antient and substantiall Inhabitants and parishoners'.[35] By contrast, they asserted that the 'cheife Ring leader of this great disorder & confusion' in opposition to Peers' election was William Powell a 'person that lately went about the County selling stockins & has [but] lately obtained a settlement' in the parish. Powell was depicted as a rabble-rouser, a person of limited substance, and (crucially) someone whose roots in the parish and commitment to its interests were shallow, compared to the wealthy, and long-resident Peers.

In this instance, a narrow minority used the idea of residence – that is, a long-standing interest in the parish – to outweigh charges that they were otherwise unrepresentative of, and unaccountable to, the community they governed. Certainly, they could demonstrate considerable geographical stability by 1713, when the average length of service of the core of the twelve most assiduous vestrymen was over sixteen years.[36] They contended that residence and wealth

32. Essex Record Office (Chelmsford) (hereafter, ERO (Chelms.)), D/Y 1/1/34, Robert Beverly to William Holman, 11 June 1723.
33. French, '"Ingenious & Learned gentlemen"', pp. 57–8
34. ERO (Chelms.), DY 1/1/97, Samuel Dale to William Holman, 11 April 1712.
35. ERO (Chelms.), Microfilm T/A 242, 'Upon notice of an appeale against the order made the last sessions', c. 1713.
36. ERO (Chelms.), D/P 264/8/2, Braintree Vestry Minutes 1655–1712.

gave them the experience and discretion to rule in the interests of all, even if they took decisions in secret, without consulting their fellow ratepayers. We tend to think of settlement and residence in the parish in connection with poor relief, as part of what Steve Hindle has termed 'the politics of entitlement'.[37] Yet, it appears that residence also formed part of the politics of entitlement to rule the parish, as well as a means of determining who should be relieved by it.

Mobility and social rank

There are two ways in which we can reconcile the extensive evidence of population turnover in specific communities with contemporaries' willingness to privilege residence and familial longevity.

The first of these can be found in Anne Mitson's evidence about the existence of 'dynastic families', not confined just to a single parish, but distributed within the normal mobility field extending for 10 or 15 miles around a particular settlement.[38] In her study of eleven contiguous Nottinghamshire parishes, although 75 per cent of the population moved out of their place of birth, most stayed within the outer boundary of the eleven parishes as a whole. In this respect, then, the magnitude of population mobility depends heavily on the scale on which we view it. From the perspective of a single parish the extent and rate of turnover appears immense. Seen in the context of a wider hinterland, the rural population begins to look more stable in geographic terms. Indeed, Mitson suggests that just as individual parishes acquired dynasties of 'stayers' (like the Goughs in Myddle), so these wider localities spawned 'dynastic families' that pushed out their root systems beyond the boundaries of a single parish. These dynasties were most notable among the ranks of the parish officers, so that between 1598 and 1710 half the churchwardens in her sample parishes came from a cluster of established families that comprised only a quarter of the general population.

This distinctive social profile adds another dimension to the findings of several other single parish studies that have identified such 'dynastic families'.[39] It also

37. Hindle, *On the Parish?*, pp. 361–449.
38. A. Mitson, 'The significance of kinship networks in the seventeenth century: south-west Nottinghamshire', in C. Phythian-Adams, ed., *Societies, Cultures and Kinship, 1580–1850: Cultural Provinces and English Local History* (Leicester, 1993), pp. 24–76.
39. G. Nair, *Highley: the Development of a Community 1550–1880* (Oxford, 1988), p. 56; B. Stapleton, 'Family strategies: patterns of inheritance in Odiham, Hampshire, 1525–1850', *Continuity and Change* 14 (1999), p. 388. Only 17 per cent of families listed in the Highley Easter Book of 1696 remained in the equivalent volume for 1744. In Odiham, while none of the forty-three long-established families were resident there throughout the period 1525–1850, twenty-seven were present for at least three generations. However, by the nineteenth century, when the community had over 2,000 inhabitants, they must have formed a tiny proportion of the total number of families.

raises the possibility that social and economic differences made some groups more mobile than others, and let the less mobile dominate the community. Unfortunately, the existing evidence for this is rather contradictory. Margaret Escott's study of Binfield, Berkshire, found that the top socio-economic group in the village (esquires, gentlemen, the wealthier farmers and tradesmen) were the *least* likely to stay in the village, with only 38 per cent remaining between 1790 and 1801, compared to 52 per cent of labourers.[40] Labourers were most likely to move *within* the parish, but were less likely to leave. Among the poor, those living in rent-free accommodation provided by the parish were the *most* likely to move (only one-third remained by 1801); those paying rent to the parish for their dwelling were the least likely to leave – four out of six remained after ten years.

Presumably these different mobility levels reflected the variations in the ability and freedom of each group to move, and much of the research into the operation of the Settlement Laws has focused on the degree to which they constrained mobility among the poor.[41] Differences in mobility levels among other social groups may reflect the proximity of new opportunities and the ability to take them up. Mitson's Nottinghamshire 'dynasties' exhibit less stability the closer their parish was to Nottingham, with the poorer, more distant communities having the most stable populations.[42] Meanwhile, in the isolated north Yorkshire village of Levisham, Betty Halse found that among her fifteen 'core' families, resident for six or more generations between 1541–1650, 'having a stake in the community in the form of agricultural land seems to have been a primary condition for long settlement of a family in the village', although this propensity declined in the

40. M. Escott, 'Residential mobility in a late eighteenth-century parish: Binfield, Berkshire 1779–1801', *Local Population Studies* 40 (1988), pp. 26–7.
41. See particularly the debate between Norma Landau and Keith Snell. N. Landau, 'The laws of settlement and the surveillance of immigration in eighteenth-century Kent', *Continuity and Change* 3 (1988), pp. 391–420; eadem, 'The regulation of immigration, economic structures and definitions of the poor in eighteenth-century England', *Hist. Jnl* 33 (1990), pp. 541–72; eadem, 'Who was subjected to the laws of settlement? Procedure under the settlement laws in eighteenth- century England', *Agricultural Hist. Rev.* 43 (1995), pp. 139–59; K. D. M. Snell, 'Pauper settlement and the right to poor relief in England and Wales', *Continuity and Change* 6 (1991), pp. 375–415; idem, 'Settlement, poor law and the rural historian: new approaches and opportunities', *Rural Hist.* 3 (1992), pp. 145–72; see also, B. Stapleton, 'Marriage, migration and mendicancy in a pre-industrial community', in B. Stapleton, ed., *Conflict and Community in Southern England: Essays in the Social History of Rural and Urban Labour from Medieval to Modern Times* (New York, 1992), pp. 51–91; R. Wells, 'Migration, the law and parochial policy in eighteenth- and early nineteenth-century southern England', *Southern Hist.* 15 (1993), pp. 86–139.
42. Mitson, 'Kinship networks', p. 61.

eighteenth century.[43] Such people may have had less reason, and perhaps less opportunity to leave than others in the community.[44]

In order to investigate these social differentials within the rates of mobility the focus will move to two different, and distant, villages – Beaminster in Dorset, and Newport Pond in Essex. Beaminster was a large parish in western Dorset, comprising six separate tithings – the villages of Beaminster and Netherbury and four surrounding hamlets of dispersed farms linked in the seventeenth and eighteenth centuries by shared common pasture downs, on which large flocks of sheep were grazed.[45] Newport Pond was in Essex, in the extreme north-west corner of the county, on the main highway between Cambridge and London. Compared to most of the rest of the county it was unusual in two respects. It was located on chalk rather than London clay, and it contained a complicated amalgam of open-field arable husbandry and common sheepwalks, alongside the enclosed farming in 'severalty' for which the rest of the county was noted.[46] Beaminster was the more populous of the two parishes. In the Dorset hearth tax of 1664, there were 303 payers in Beaminster, compared to 130 payers in Newport one year earlier.[47]

While these two communities were very different in terms of topography, agrarian practice and settlement patterns, they share one archival feature. Both have series of parish rates at annual intervals for much of the seventeenth century. For Beaminster there is a contiguous series from 1647 to 1719 (with gaps in 1661–3 and 1705–10); for Newport there are rates (usually more than one) every year between 1661 and 1720. These series give an unrivalled opportunity for us to examine stability and mobility among the rate-paying population.[48]

43. B. Halse, 'Population mobility in the village of Levisham, 1541–1900', *Local Population Studies* 65 (2000), pp. 60–2.
44. Of course, the preservation of *families* within a settlement could be at the expense of younger children, who were often more likely be mobile than their eldest sibling, because they were usually denied the resources necessary to establish an 'ecological niche' in their home parish, particularly in farming families.
45. G. E. Fussell, 'Four centuries of farming systems in Dorset, 1500–1900', *Proc. Dorset Natural Hist. and Arch. Soc.* 73 (1952), pp. 119, 127–8; J. H. Bettey, 'Land tenure and manorial custom in Dorset 1570–1670', *Southern Hist.* 4 (1982), pp. 33–54.
46. J. Thirsk, ed., *The Agrarian History of England and Wales Vol. V 1640–1750: I. Regional Farming Systems* (Cambridge, 1984), pp. 206–7, 210–11.
47. C. A. F. Meekings, *Dorset Hearth Tax Assessments 1662–1664* (Dorchester, 1951); ERO (Chelms.), D/P 15/8/1, Newport Parish Book, 1659–1706, f. 17.
48. This approach requires the transcription of all rates in the series and the calculation of the indexed median figure for each person in each year of the sample. While this is a simple process electronically, it involves a large amount of data. The Beaminster rate sample contains approximately 12,000 entries between 1630 and 1719, while the Newport Pond rates amount to approximately 15,500 entries between 1661 and 1720.

Table 4.2 Comparison of the percentages of ratepayers remaining, in years after 1662 for ratepayers assessed and not assessed on the hearth tax, in Newport Pond, Essex and Beaminster, Dorset

1662 ratepayers	No. in group	Years after 1662							
		5	10	15	20	25	30	35	40
Newport Pond, Essex									
Assessed in 1662 Hearth Tax	73	77	69	58	45	33	26	16	14
Not assessed in 1662 Tax	30	60	40	20	13	13	13	7	7
Beaminster, Dorset									
Assessed in 1664 Hearth Tax	59	73	64	53	44	29	24	15	10
Not assessed in 1664 Tax	35	51	46	23	20	6	6	3	3

Sources: C. A. F. Meekings, *Dorset Hearth Tax Assessments 1662–1664* (Dorchester, 1951); ERO (Chelms.), D/P 15/8/1, Newport Parish Book, 1659–1706, f. 17; Dorset RO, MIC/R/1335, Beaminster Churchwardens' Account Book 1646–1712.

However, there are a number of problems in the use of rates for this purpose. Obviously, they tell us only about the rate-paying section of society, not the 40 or 50 per cent of people exempt from such assessments. Without equally comprehensive Easter listings of communicants or lists of poor relief recipients, it is impossible to reconstruct settlement patterns among other sections of the village. In addition, rates, like manorial rentals, do not demonstrate who was *actually* resident. Instead, they show who paid, or was expected to pay, the assessment. Therefore, it is dangerous to assume that rate payment equates to occupation of the property in all cases. Third, like rentals, rates refer to all properties on which rates were paid, not merely residential ones. Therefore, some ratepayers were simply landowners in a parish, and may have had no residence there. It becomes difficult in such circumstances to disentangle the length of ownership or leasing of land from length of residence in a parish.

One way of overcoming some of these problems is to compare these series of rates with the hearth tax for these two communities. While such a comparison does not guarantee that we will be dealing only with resident ratepayers, it does allow us to sift out many of the non-resident, non-householding occupiers of land. Table 4.2 illustrates this comparison for the two sample parishes. Of the two, Newport has the closest 'fit' between the rate-paying and hearth-tax-paying populations, with only eighteen out of ninety-one of the hearth-taxpayers in 1662 missing from the parish rates. In Beaminster the picture is much less clear, with only sixty-seven out of the 187 ratepayers in 1661 appearing on the 1662–4 hearth tax listing. Despite these variations, both parishes suggest that hearth-taxpayers were likely to pay rates for longer than ratepayers who do not feature on the tax, and who therefore might not have been resident in each of these settlements. In both parishes twenty years after the datum point of 1662 double the percentage of hearth-taxpayers remained compared to the non-hearth-taxpayers.

If we compare the figures for the percentage of hearth-taxpayers remaining in the parish rates after 1662, as shown in Table 4.2, we can see that both the proportions, and the length of time that these payers remained in their communities appear very similar. After ten years, just over 60 per cent remained in the rates, after twenty years just over 40 per cent, after thirty years, around 25 per cent remained. Given the broad similarity of the first figure with those given in Table 4.1, we might have some confidence in the reliability of these proportions – even if they do not refer to the majority of the population, and in the absence of full family reconstructions, are necessarily imprecise. In this respect, then, while such rate series probably include a number of non-residents, they do give a useful insight into the turnover of a section of the more prosperous householders in the village – a section from which Richard Gough was drawn.

Persistence of families

Were there differences in the length of residence of particular groups of ratepayers in these two parishes, in the same way that there appeared to be differences between the groups of ratepayers who paid the hearth tax and those who did not?

My previous research with Richard Hoyle on Earls Colne showed how officers and attendees of the vestry paid rates for *four* times the median number of years for non-office-holding ratepayers.[49] It also demonstrated that this stability may have been a function of their greater longevity as copyholders – they and their families were much more likely to be copyholders, and held land on average for twice as long as the non-office-holding ratepayers.[50] Earls Colne provides some support for Halse's notion that landholding was a factor that affected length of residence in a community. It also suggests that this could contribute to the creation of a group of 'dynastic' families who exerted considerable influence over their community, in the ways that Mitson has suggested. Newport and Beaminster exhibit similar kinds of divisions in terms of length of residence between ratepayers who were or were not officeholders.

Table 4.3 examines the length of time over which the 1690 cohort of ratepayers paid rates, in the years before and after this datum point. Such an analysis allows a longer perspective on the ratepaying careers of this group than would be possible simply by looking *forward* from a particular date. The cohort is divided into two

49. This research was incorporated in H. R. French, 'Social status, localism and the "middle sort of people" in England 1620–1750', *Past and Present* 166 (2000), pp. 88–93. A fuller treatment of office and status in Earls Colne can be found in H. R. French and R. W. Hoyle, *The Character of English Rural Society, 1550–1750: Earls Colne Revisited* (Manchester, 2006), Chapter 8.
50. In Earls Colne, between 1722 and 1750 only one-fifth of the non-office-holding ratepayers (twenty-five out of 127) were copyholders. In the same period half the officers and vestrymen were copyholders (forty-six out of ninety-two). French, 'Social status', Table 10.

Table 4.3 Comparison of the percentages of 1690 cohort of ratepayers who were either officers and vestrymen, or never officers, remaining in rates before or after 1690, Newport Pond and Beaminster

1690 ratepayers	N	Years pre-1690						Years post-1690					
		30	25	20	15	10	5	5	10	15	20	25	30
Newport Pond													
Officers	54	26	41	44	59	67	85	78	54	41	30	20	17
Non-officers	24	13	21	33	38	42	46	42	29	21	13	8	4
Beaminster													
Officers	59	25	29	34	39	61	86	90	66	59	58	39	32
Non-officers	90	14	17	19	23	37	62	73	52	44	41	28	19

Sources: ERO (Chelms.), D/P 15/8/1, Newport Parish Book, 1659–1706, D/P/ 15/8/9 Newport Parish Book 1706–1939; Dorset RO, MIC/R/1335, Beaminster Churchwardens' Account Book 1646–1712.

groups in the period between 1660 and 1720: those who served in parish office, and those who appear never to have done so. As can be seen, in *both* parishes in the thirty-year periods both before and after 1690 those who served in parish office or who attended the vestry meeting were much more likely to remain as ratepayers in the settlement. Except in Beaminster after 1690, more than *twice* the proportion of officers and vestrymen remained in these parishes after thirty years, compared to the non-officers. Some of this variation may be due to a portion of the latter group not being physically resident in these settlements, compared to officers (who were supposed to serve in the parishes in which they resided). Even so, the greater apparent stability of these parish officers is quite striking.

Figures 4.2 to 4.5 depict the length of time over which the individual officers and non-officers in these two sample parishes paid rates, and illustrate the patterns that underlie these percentages. In Newport Pond, forty-five out of fifty-four officers (83 per cent) paid rates in a period of twenty or more years – or forty-three (80 per cent) if we discount two names that appear across all sixty years. In Beaminster, forty-seven out of fifty-nine (80 per cent) of officers did so. By contrast, only 46 and 63 per cent of non-officers paid over a period of twenty or more years.[51] In other respects, the groups were distributed relatively evenly, with approximately one-third near the end of their ratepaying careers, one-third in mid-career and one-third near the beginning of their term as ratepayers in 1690.[52] The

51. That is, eleven out of twenty-four non-office-holding ratepayers in Newport Pond, and fifty-seven out of ninety in Beaminster.
52. Among officers and vestrymen in Newport Pond twenty-two were near the end of their time as ratepayers, fifteen were in mid-career, and seventeen were near the beginning. Among non-officers in the parish, the figures were nine, eight and seven respectively. In Beaminster, fifteen officers and vestrymen were near the end of their time as ratepayers in 1690, twenty-two were in mid-career, and twenty-two were near the beginning. Among non-officers, the figures were twenty, twenty-four and forty-five respectively – the last figure being the only disproportionate one in the series.

Table 4.4 Median index 'lifetime' rate payments for officer and non-officer ratepayers in 1690 ratepaying cohort, Newport Pond and Beaminster (where parish median = 100)

	Officers	Non-officers
Newport Pond	142.2	63.9
Beaminster	50.6	27.9

Sources: ERO (Chelms.), D/P 15/8/1, Newport Parish Book, 1659–1706, D/P/ 15/8/9 Newport Parish Book 1706–1939; Dorset RO, MIC/R/1335, Beaminster Churchwardens' Account Book 1646–1712.

exception to this pattern was in Beaminster, where there seems to have been an influx of (long-term) new payers in the 1680s, of whom most never served in parish office in subsequent years.

Table 4.4 illustrates the disparities in the rate assessments levied on the two groups in both parishes. The figures represent a composite index figure – where each assessment in each rate in the series has been indexed as a proportion of the parish median for that particular rate – so that where the parish median is, say, 4d., the indexed figure for a rate assessment of 6d. will be 150 (per cent of 4d.). The medians of each of these annual indexed figures have been compiled for each payer for both parishes to give a final 'lifetime' median assessment. The medians of these 'lifetime' assessments have then been calculated for ratepayers in the two groups, of officers and non-officers in the two parishes, and are depicted in the table. These show that in *both* parishes officers were likely to be assessed at over twice the rate levels of non-officers through their ratepaying careers, even if both groups remained well below the median for the whole parish in Beaminster. This confirms and extends the earlier research conclusions based on Earls Colne, and suggests that the officers of the parish were more likely to be of long standing, and of greater wealth than their less influential neighbours – as was obviously the case in Myddle also.

Such analyses begin to disclose the aggregate differences in wealth and opportunities, as well as to hint at the individual differences in character and fortune that lay beneath the patterns of persistence or mobility in village life, as depicted so vividly by Richard Gough. It is also interesting that Myddle appears to have conformed so fully to these patterns – exemplifying how the wealthy, office-holding parochial elite provided the most geographically stable section of the community. Yet, there was a profound difference between having been long resident in a parish in *one* lifetime, and having the family background necessary to be another Richard Gough – able to draw on the memories of three or four generations.

How many ratepayers had the potential to be another Richard Gough? This is extremely difficult to determine, without the 'ideal' combination of an extensive

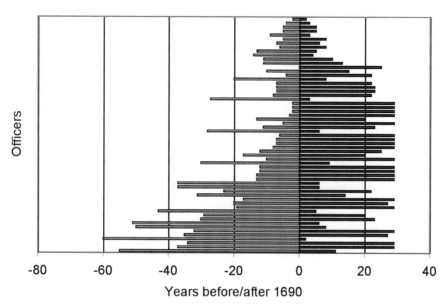

Figure 4.2 Beaminster, 1630–1719: years over which 1690 cohort of officeholding ratepayers paid rates (N=54)

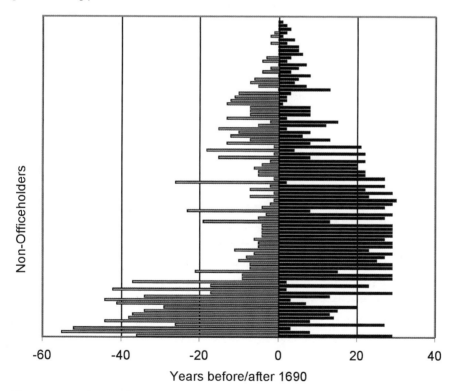

Figure 4.3 Beaminster, 1630–1719: years over which 1690 cohort of non-officeholding ratepayers paid rates (N=90)

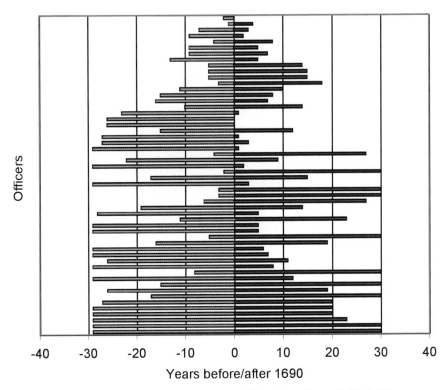

Figure 4.4 Newport Pond, 1661–1720: years over which 1690 cohort of officeholding ratepayers paid rates (N=54)

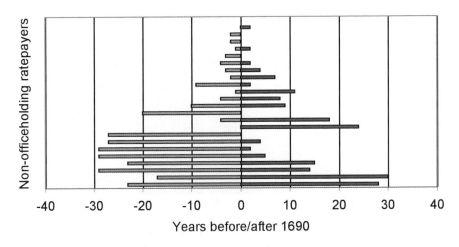

Figure 4.5 Newport Pond, 1661–1720: years over which 1690 cohort of non-officeholding ratepayers paid rates (N=24)

series of rates, in a parish that also possesses a comprehensive family reconstitution. At present, the best we can do is to return to the Essex village of Earls Colne, and the extensive electronic archive amassed by Alan Macfarlane and his team of researchers.[53] The indexes of this archive enable the historian to trace all the records of an individual back to his or her birth or first documented mention in the parish. For natives of the village, these indexes also provide interactive links to the parental generation (through names in the baptismal record), and so on back to earlier generations, where those individuals were also resident in the village. Such links give us a brief, and rudimentary glimpse of the kinds of genealogies that Richard Gough carried around in his head.

In October 1750 there were sixty-eight ratepayers in Earls Colne.[54] Of these, the available evidence suggests that twenty-five were born in the village. In the rate series extending back to 1722, these twenty-five paid rates over a median period of eighteen years, compared to ten years among the forty-three non-native ratepayers. This small disparity conceals the much larger one that appears when all the records relating to each individual are searched, to find the date of the first record relating to that person. Among non-natives, the length of residence is stretched to a median of twelve years. As might be expected, among natives (whose baptisms are registered in the parish), this extends dramatically, to a median of forty-five years – showing the median age of this group as a whole. Despite this difference, only a minority of the sixty-eight ratepayers could demonstrate a lineage to rival Richard Gough's. Of the natives, five possessed a paternal or maternal lineage in the village extending back to the first half of the seventeenth century, over four or five generations. Among these, Thomas Hales was the closest equivalent to Richard Gough, since his great-grandfather, Thomas Hales the first, had bought their family farm in 1611.[55] This estate had descended through four generations of male heirs (all called Thomas) to Thomas the fifth, who held it in 1750. Thomas' brother-in-law, John Osborn, possessed direct ancestors in the village back to 1636.[56] John Newton, a wealthy copyholder, seems only to have been able to trace his father's family in the village to 1673, but his

53. These Earls Colne materials are accessible on Macfarlane's personal website: <http://www.alanmacfarlane.com>.
54. ERO (Chelms.), D/P 209/8, Earls Colne Poor Rate, 1 October 1750 [11402520 – website document reference].
55. ERO (Chelms.), D/DPr 21, Colne Priory Manor Court Rolls 22 Mar. 1611 [33400477].
56. ERO (Chelms.), D/DPr 100, Earls Colne Manor Fine Book 1636 [24003282]. For familial relationship, see D/ACW27 OSBORNE and D/ACR 14/383 will of Edmund Osborne, 1730 [5800509].

mother's extended to 1605.[57] John White Jr. and Plampin Wenden could trace their maternal lines back to 1648 and 1628 respectively.[58] There were a few potential Goughs, too, among those ratepayers without a baptism in the parish. Oliver Johnson had married the heir to the Abbott family, wealthy residents of the village since at least 1564, whose antics would have provided Gough with a fund of stories.[59] The lord of the manor, John Wale, could trace his ancestry back through his mother's family to the Harlakendens, who had bought the parish's two manors in 1583 and 1592.[60] The lord was outdone by Grace Hatch, who had inherited her father's copyhold house in 1746, but whose paternal family extended back directly to 1603, and through the maternal line to 1577.[61]

Such individuals exercised due influence in the affairs of Earls Colne. Fourteen of the twenty-five native ratepayers had served in parish office or as vestrymen between 1722 and 1750, and therefore comprised just under one-third of the thirty-three ratepayers in the 1750 cohort who had done so in this period. Despite their involvement, they were assisted in government of the parish by a large number of newcomers. George Fromont (master of the grammar school) had arrived in 1736,[62] the surgeon Samuel Smith in 1740,[63] Richard Ruffle (son-in-law of John Newton) in 1742,[64] and Thomas Pascall, the tenant to a large (140-acre)

57. ERO (Chelms.), D/DPr 100, Earls Colne Manor Fine Book 1673 [23800896]. His mother's family, the Potters, can be traced to James Potter, who died in 1605, TNA: PRO, PROB 11/117/404v will of James Potter [3302033].

58. ERO (Chelms.), D/P 209/2, Earls Colne Baptism Register 1640–9, 14 February 1648, first reference to John Isaacson, father of John White Jr.'s grandmother Margery (b. 1656) [6802737]; Wenden's great-grandmother Dorothy was first recorded in ERO (Chelms.), D/ACW 11/3, John Potter Sr, will dated 12 June 1628 [3900802].

59. Johnson's wife Abigail was the heir to the Abbott family in Earls Colne. Her great-great-grandfather, Henry, was baptised in the parish in March 1564, ERO (Chelms.), D/P 209/1/1, Earls Colne Baptism Register 1560–99 [6500582].

60. The Harlakendens' first recorded involvement with the parish was in 1579, when Richard Harlakenden took a lease of the demesne from the then lord, the Earl of Oxford, ERO (Chelms.), D/Q 6/2/2, Freehold Titles 29 September 1579 [32400352].

61. Grace's great-great grandfather, John Hatch, married Rachel Hayward in May 1603, ERO (Chelms.), D/P 209/1/1, Earls Colne Marriage Register 1600–5 [8900141]; Rachel's brother, Richard, was recorded as baptised in the parish in August 1577. ERO (Chelms.) Earls Colne Baptism Register 1560–99 [6502914].

62. ERO (Chelms.), D/P 209/14/1, Apprenticeship Indenture, 10 November 1736 [11802423] (Fromont acts as witness). Fromont was described as 'schoolmaster' aged twenty-nine years on his marriage licence, granted in September 1740, ERO (Chelms.), D/ALL, Marriage Bonds and Allegations 1672–1750 [10500593].

63. ERO (Chelms.), D/DPr 100A, Colne Priory Manor Fine Book 1740 [23903337]. There were two Samuel Smiths in the village at this time. The other, Samuel Smith, farmer, was born there in 1684, ERO (Chelms.), D/P 209/1/3, Earls Colne Baptism Register 1680–89 [7201285].

64. ERO (Chelms.), D/ACL Box 3, Marriage Bonds and Allegations, 26 January 1742 [10301199]. Richard Ruffle, of Wickham St Pauls, farmer, aged twenty-three to marry Hannah Newton of Earls Colne.

leasehold farm, only in 1747.[65] Of the forty-three incoming ratepayers, who had
not been chosen to parish office, twenty-six had first appeared in the 1730s and
1740s. Earls Colne's more prosperous inhabitants bear out Laslett's 'startling
fact'. Natives of the village were outnumbered by two to one among the rate-
paying householders, and the eight families who had roots extending back over
three or four generations, stood as isolated points of continuity amid the flux of
constant population turnover. If we were able to locate them among the non-ratepaying population no doubt they would appear all the more unusual.

Eighteenth-century Earls Colne probably possessed a less settled population
than Myddle did in Gough's lifetime. Although almost half the land in Earls
Colne's two manors continued to be held by small or medium copyholders,
perhaps half of those landholders rented out their properties to sub-tenants. Most
of the remaining land (the lord's demesnes, and freehold farms sold off from
these demesnes) was also rented out, creating opportunities for short-term
tenancies, and thinning out the ranks of the owner-occupying yeoman-farmers.[66]
This contrasted with Gough's village, where owner-occupation and dynastic
descent was favoured by the system of three-life leases or copyholds, and by those
prudent enough to buy from the Earl of Bridgewater in the middle of the
seventeenth century. As Hey points out, though, this situation changed shortly
after Gough's death in 1723, as the Bridgewater estate expanded again, and most
of the old yeoman families sold out, to be replaced by more mobile and non-native
tenant-farmers.[67] By 1750, the population in Myddle was probably closer in its
composition and the shallowness of its roots to that found in Earls Colne.

Conclusion

In these respects, then, while most villages were likely to have contained their
versions of the Goughs, these dynasties seem likely always to have constituted a
tiny minority of the residents at any single point in time. No doubt, such 'antient
families' could command additional respect by displaying the length of their
ancestry and the breadth of their local knowledge. However, their rarity may have
meant that for most parochial rulers (and would-be rulers) it was enough simply

65. ERO (Chelms.), D/P 209/8, Earls Colne Poor Rate 20 Apr. 1747 [11400039].58. ERO (Chelms.),
    D/P 209/2, Earls Colne Baptism Register 1640–9, 14 February 1648, first reference to John
    Isaacson, father of John White Jr.'s grandmother Margery (b. 1656) [6802737]; Wenden's great-
    grandmother Dorothy was first recorded in ERO (Chelms.), D/ACW 11/3, John Potter Sr, will
    dated 12 June 1628 [3900802].
66. H. R. French and R. W. Hoyle, 'English Individualism refuted – and reasserted: the land market of
    Earls Colne (Essex), 1550–1750', Econ. Hist. Rev. 61 (2003), pp. 616–17.
67. Hey, English Rural Community, pp. 11, 83.

to count as 'antient inhabitants' – long resident in one lifetime, rather than several. The vestry meeting in Earls Colne was composed primarily of longer-term ratepayers, supplemented by one or two 'antient families', plus a fair sprinkling of prosperous newcomers, the 'substantial inhabitants' of the parish. Increasingly, 'antient' status may have reflected the payment of rates over fifteen or twenty years rather than over five, instead of residence over five generations rather than one.

This division between 'ancient' and other inhabitants occurred even in the crowded and highly mobile confines of London parish life. Julia Merritt has noted that the parish rulers of Westminster described themselves repeatedly in this period as the 'ancients of the parish'.[68] She suggests that this term became synonymous with membership of the parish vestry. A 1696 petition against 'select' (restricted) vestries objected that such vestrymen often assumed 'to themselves the name of Ancients'.[69] It was even worth recording on one's tombstone. Richard Bedoe of St Clement Danes was immortalised as 'one of the ancientest of this parish'.[70] This was a euphemism for power in the community, but it also reflected a practical reality – without long residence, the long-term exercise of power was impossible. However, given the extensive mobility (and high mortality levels) within London, those who maintained residential stability were particularly able to accumulate authority over their neighbours. As elsewhere, this stability was probably also a function of their greater wealth.

This variety of experiences allows us to begin to reconcile the two contrasting stories that historians tell about life in the 'self-contained village', by showing that these differing accounts are compatible with each other, because they relate to different groups within the parish. We are confronted with abundant evidence of the mobility of those at the level of the ordinary ratepayers, and (apparently) among the non-ratepaying labouring poor. For them, it is clear that the parish of birth was not necessarily the prime focus of their chances in life (in work, landholding and housing, let alone family, marriage partners, kin and 'friends'). While most single-parish studies indicate that the landholding, social networks and positions of authority of those near the top of the parish hierarchy were not confined within the bounds of a single community, this research suggests that these families might remain resident longer in a settlement than the bulk of parishioners *within* one generation, and sometimes across several generations. Similarly, studies of poor relief have indicated that within a single generation

68. J. F. Merritt, *The Social World of Early Modern Westminster Abbey, Court and Community, 1525–1640* (Manchester, 2005), pp. 137, 213.
69. Ibid., p. 137.
70. Ibid., p. 213.

those in regular receipt of poor relief might be tethered to the parish, as settled but not entirely voluntary residents.[71]

This routine mobility is not necessarily incompatible with Keith Snell's recent work on 'local xenophobia', and its emphasis on the distinct 'cultures' that might exist within individual parishes, often in contrast to (and conflict with) those of their neighbours. The important point is not that people *did not* move between parishes, but rather that when they did, they had to *assimilate* to the norms, customs, values and activities of those who were already resident, or run the gauntlet of the many forms of sanction levied against the incomer. As long as each generation possessed a core of long-term residents to maintain continuity, transfer local knowledge and secure conformity, the extensive turnover of population between parishes would not disturb this cultural transmission – loyalties might be acquired and enacted, rather than being wholly innate (see pp. 22, 27). In this sense, the upheavals of enclosure or estate building that effected fundamental change in land use, life and custom may have been more corrosive to the 'self-contained' cultures of the parish than the fact of short-range population mobility itself.

This interpretation helps to explain how village 'culture' could persist despite the rapid turnover of its participants. However, it does not resolve a further historical paradox. While Laslett and his successors have disproved the assumption that we are divided from the inhabitants of the 'World We Have Lost' because we are mobile and they were not, they have also exposed how we are united with them in the belief that village life *should* somehow represent an idyll of organic, unchanging and enduring 'community' and residence, and that it *did* so in the past. The roots of this myth can be found in Richard Gough's selective memory, as it winnowed out the 'stayers' from the chaff thrown up by mobility and mortality in his village. This stable minority formed the core of his *History*, because they impressed themselves most firmly on his memory, in the same way that they figure most strongly in parochial or manorial sources upon which we base our histories of the 'self-contained village' today. In view of this, while we may hear the stories told in the authoritative tones of the 'antientest and most substantiall' inhabitants better than the fainter fragments left by their neighbours who came and went, these shorter tales are just as representative of life in these communities in the period covered in this chapter.

---

71. In addition to the debate between Snell and Landau mentioned in Note 41 above, see also Hindle, *On the Parish?*, pp. 311–26, 337–60.

5

Cumbrian village communities: continuity and change, c.1750–c.1850

IAN WHYTE

Cumbria has been described as the 'odd corner' of England, a region in which rural society was 150 years behind the rest of the country, preserving elements of feudalism and a peasant economy into the late eighteenth century and beyond.[1] Rents in kind and labour, customary fines and heriots were still a feature of many Cumbrian manors in the eighteenth century.[2] This image of backwardness has been seen as a defining characteristic of the region.[3] Cumbria, and its rural society, have not always been taken on their own terms, part of a wider tendency, criticised in recent years by Christopher Smout and Angus Winchester, for many social, economic and landscape historians to view the area from a southern-based perspective.[4] As a result of this, less research has been done on the structure of Cumbrian communities and how they changed over time than for most parts of England.

Despite some important research on the society and economy of Cumbrian communities during the seventeenth and eighteenth centuries, many important questions remain unanswered.[5] In a society in which access to land was more

1. C. E. Searle, 'The odd corner of England: a study of a rural social formation in transition. Cumbria c. 1700–1914' (unpublished Ph.D., Essex, 1983).
2. C. E. Searle, 'Custom, class conflict and agrarian capitalism. The Cumbrian customary economy in the eighteenth century', *Past and Present* 110 (1986), pp. 106–33.
3. Searle, 'Odd corner', pp. 15–16.
4. T. C. Smout, *Nature Contested: Environmental History in Scotland and Northern England since 1600* (Edinburgh, 2000), pp. 12–20; A. J. L. Winchester, *The Harvest of the Hills: Rural Life in Northern England and the Scottish Borders, 1400–1700* (Edinburgh, 2000), pp. 3–4.
5. See, for example, G. P. Jones, 'The decline of the yeomanry in the Lake Counties', *Trans. Cumberland and Westmorland Antiq. and Arch. Soc.* 62 (1962), pp. 198–223; J. D. Marshall, 'The domestic economy of the Lakeland yeoman 1660–1740', *Trans. Cumberland and Westmorland Antiq. and Arch. Soc.* 73 (1973), pp. 190–219; J. D. Marshall, 'Agrarian wealth and social structure in pre-industrial Cumbria', *Econ. Hist. Rev.* 33 (1980), pp. 503–21; J. K. Walton, 'The strange decline of the Lake District yeoman: some thoughts on sources, methods and definitions', *Trans. Cumberland and Westmorland Antiq. and Arch. Soc.* 86 (1986), pp. 221–33; A. J. L. Winchester, 'Wordsworth's "pure commonwealth"? Yeoman dynasties in the English Lake District c. 1450–1750', *Armitt Library Jnl* 1 (1998), pp. 86–113.

Figure 5.1 Milburn, Westmorland. Located at the foot of the Cross Fell escarpment, Milburn, with its rectangular green, epitomises the regularly planned villages of the Eden valley (Photograph by Ian Whyte)

widespread than in most parts of England, how significant was the landless element at various periods? What role did the extensive areas of common manorial waste play in the economies of village communities, especially with regard to the poorer elements of society? How were the social structures of village communities affected by the rise of agrarian capitalism in the eighteenth century? Of particular concern here were the impacts on Cumbrian society of the rapid social and economic changes which occurred in the late eighteenth and early nineteenth centuries. One of these, parliamentary enclosure, has been associated in other parts of England with the transformation of self-contained rural social structures as well as with the spread of modernity and market forces in agriculture.[6] To what extent did Cumbrian communities fit in with the concept of the self-contained village and how did they change between the later eighteenth and mid-nineteenth centuries? The aim of this chapter is to explore some of these issues, offer some suggestions, and point to some potentially profitable directions for future research.

6.   The literature on parliamentary enclosure in England is enormous. For recent contributions to the debate see: R. C. Allen, *Enclosure and the Yeomen: The Agricultural Development of the South Midlands 1450–1850* (Oxford, 1992); J. Neeson, *Commoners: Common Right, Enclosure and Social Change in England 1700–1870* (Cambridge, 1993); M. Overton, *Agricultural Revolution in England. The Transformation of the Agrarian Economy 1500–1850* (Cambridge, 1996).

This study uses a range of data relating to Cumbrian village communities, mainly ones from the upper Eden and Lune valleys in northern Westmorland, the most upland of all English counties. This area is classic northern village country. Many of the nucleated villages have regular plans, laid out in parallel rows facing central greens, dating from the period following the Norman annexation of Cumbria in 1092.[7] (Figure 5.1) While there was some medieval creation of new farms on intakes of land beyond the village open fields, in many townships at the time of parliamentary enclosure most of the farms were still located within the main settlements.

These villages had originally been associated with common field systems, often laid out in long tofts, the aratral curves of which can still be discerned in the modern landscape from the patterns of later enclosure boundaries.[8] However, enclosure by private agreement from late medieval times had removed many common fields entirely and reduced others to mere vestiges. A similar process had occurred with common meadows, so that by the mid-eighteenth century the only category of communal land associated with many Cumbrian villages was the manorial waste.[9] The management and fate of the commons in the eighteenth century were of central importance to the continuation of local self-sufficiency.

Rural society in Cumbria in the seventeenth and early eighteenth centuries

Cumbria, in the seventeenth and eighteenth centuries, preserved a distinctive structure of rural society based on the prevalence of customary tenure which, while retaining elements of feudalism, gave tenants rights regarding the disposal of their lands which were effectively equivalent to freehold, together with rents which had failed to keep place with inflation. These rights stemmed from pre-seventeenth-century Border tenures in which security of occupation was granted in return for military service against the Scots.[10] The continuation of these rights had been acknowledged by the courts in various test cases during the seventeenth and

7. B. K. Roberts, 'Norman village plantation and long strip fields in Northern England,' *Geografiska Annaler* 70b (1988), pp. 169–77; B. K. Roberts, 'Five Westmorland settlements: a comparative study', *Trans. Cumberland and Westmorland Antiq. and Arch. Soc.* 93 (1993), pp. 331–45.

8. B. K. Roberts, 'The great plough: a hypothesis concerning village genesis and land reclamation in Cumberland and Westmorland', *Landscape Hist.* 18 (1996), pp. 17–30.

9. G. Elliott, 'Field systems of northwest England', in A. R. H. Baker and R. A. Butlin, eds, *Studies of Field Systems in the British Isles* (Cambridge, 1973), pp. 76–84; B. Tyson, 'Murton great field near Appleby: a case study of the piecemeal enclosure of a common field in the mid-eighteenth century', *Trans. Cumberland and Westmorland Antiq. and Arch. Soc.* 92 (1992), pp. 161–82.

10. R. W. Hoyle, 'An ancient and laudable custom: the definition and development of tenant right in north western England in the sixteenth century', *Past and Present* 116 (1987), pp. 24–55.

eighteenth centuries.[11] Customary tenants still held between a third and two-thirds of the land in Cumbrian manors during the eighteenth century.[12] The key feature of Cumbrian society was the persistence of this class of small, independent owner-occupiers and their family farms into the eighteenth century or even later.[13] The widespread survival of small peasant holdings with a limited market orientation tended to reinforce self-sufficiency at family and community levels. As a result of this pattern of small farms, relatively few wage labourers were employed.[14] Most of the farm work was done by living-in servants and, especially, by family members. Although customary tenants generally occupied holdings with under 50 acres,[15] most of them also had access to extensive commons. Only in the southern part of the Lake District is there likely to have been a substantial landless element in the population due to employment in woodland industries, iron smelting and domestic textile manufacture.[16]

Between the mid-seventeenth and mid-eighteenth centuries Cumbrian yeomen as a class had enjoyed modest prosperity and there had been little decline in their overall numbers.[17] As well as profits from the cattle droving trade this prosperity has been linked to modest levels of customary fines, low land tax assessments and the existence of a range of by-employments outside agriculture.[18] This group continued to display signs of prosperity in the late eighteenth and early nineteenth centuries: their numbers and the strength of their traditional tenures had the effect of limiting the power of manorial lords and their ability to develop a more commercialised agrarian economy.[19]

At a county level Cumbrian society was characterised by the lack of a resident aristocracy and a higher gentry group as most such families were absentees.[20] At the village level the larger customary tenants, who were usually described in

11. Winchester, 'Pure commonwealth', pp. 86–113; Searle, 'Customary economy', pp. 106–33.
12. Searle, 'Customary economy', p. 128.
13. Winchester, 'Pure commonwealth', p. 88.
14. Searle, 'Odd corner', p. 49.
15. Marshall, 'Agrarian wealth', p. 202; Searle, 'Odd corner', pp. 54, 68.
16. Winchester, 'Pure commonwealth', p. 92.
17. Marshall, 'Agrarian wealth', pp. 503–21.
18. J. V. Beckett, 'The decline of the small landowner in eighteenth- and nineteenth-century England: some regional considerations', *Agric. Hist. Rev.* 30 (1982), pp. 97–111. C. E. Searle, 'Customary tenants and the enclosure of the Cumbrian commons', *Northern Hist.* 29 (1993), pp. 129–24.
19. N. Gregson, 'Tawney revisited: custom and the emergence of capitalist class relations in north east Cumbria 1600–1830', *Econ. Hist. Rev.*, 2nd ser. 42 (1989), pp. 18–42. C. E. Searle, 'Cumbria's parliamentary enclosure movement: a comparative case study in rural quiescence', *Trans. Cumberland and Westmorland Antiq. and Arch. Soc.* 95 (1995), pp. 247–69.
20. Winchester, 'Pure commonwealth', p. 91.

contemporary documents as yeomen, intermarried with gentry families and often held most of the important local offices.[21] While there were doubtless many subtle gradations within the ranks of the customary tenants, in the seventeenth century at least they seem to have possessed a good deal of group solidarity, something which is demonstrated by their successful concerted opposition to attempts by their landlords to downgrade their tenures.[22] At the community level the pattern of land occupation could be more complex than has been outlined here. For example, the extent to which land was sub-let by the larger customary tenants is far from clear. Some smaller estates, as well as larger ones, were held in freehold. In the course of the seventeenth century the inhabitants of some villages, such as Orton, bought out their manorial rights and thus had an even greater measure of independence.[23] At the bottom of the spectrum of landholding there was a good deal of squatting and encroachment on the commons in areas like Cartmel and Inglewood Forest during the period of population pressure which marked the late sixteenth and early seventeenth centuries.[24] In some areas this continued to be a problem in the eighteenth century.[25] The huge extent of many commons encouraged manorial courts to tolerate such encroachments. The squatters derived some benefit from grazing livestock on the wastes, from collecting fuel and from exploiting other common resources. So, in the seventeenth century, did the completely landless element in Westmorland villages. As grazing rights on the common were dependent on the occupation of land within the manor, landless cottagers and labourers, strictly speaking, should not have had access to pasture. Manorial court records indicate, however, that local interpretations of this rule were sometimes more flexible.[26] In the course of the eighteenth century, though, manorial courts displayed a hardening of attitudes to the use of commons by such people, placing increasing restrictions on their activities.[27] This process is in line with Shaw-Taylor's findings for parts of southern England.[28]

By the middle of the eighteenth century there were signs of stress within Cumbrian village communities associated with a trend towards growing social differentiation and widening gaps in prosperity. The interests of the larger

21. Winchester, 'Pure commonwealth', pp. 93, 97.
22. Searle, 'Customary economy', pp. 111–12.
23. I. D. Whyte, *Transforming Fell and Valley: Landscape and Parliamentary Enclosure in North West England* (Lancaster, 2003), p. 58.
24. A. B. Appleby, *Famine in Tudor and Stuart England* (Liverpool, 1978); J. Stockdale, *Annals of Cartmel* (Ulverston, 1872), pp. 197–8.
25. Stockdale, *Cartmel*, pp. 197–9.
26. Winchester, *Harvest of the Hills*, pp. 74–84.
27. Searle, 'Parliamentary enclosure movement', p. 264.
28. L. Shaw-Taylor, 'Parliamentary enclosure and the emergence of an English agricultural proletariat', *Jnl Econ. Hist.* 61 (2002), pp. 640–62.

customary tenants were starting to diverge from those of their smaller neighbours in the face of both internal and external pressures which focused particularly on the management of the commons. The regulation of these by manorial courts became increasingly difficult due to the impact of the cattle trade. Although it was possible to engage in the cattle trade on a small scale it appears to have been the large proprietors, with extensive demesnes, and the bigger customary tenants, who really benefited. The profits from fattening and re-selling lean Scottish cattle encouraged larger tenants to overgraze the commons by exceeding their stints or ignoring the custom of levancy and couchancy which required them to graze no more animals on the commons in summer than they could winter on their inbye (improved) land.[29] Larger customary tenants increasingly rode roughshod over manorial custom by defying the manorial courts. On some commons they virtually monopolised access to the pastures, preventing small tenants from exercising their rights at all or harassing them when they tried to do so. 'Dogging', using dogs to drive a neighbour's livestock from the best grazings, or even right off the common, was a widespread practice.[30] The smaller customary tenants then were being excluded from the commons or, if continuing to use them, were seeing their value decline due to over-use and lack of control. In such circumstances it is unlikely that the grazing of animals by landless labourers and cottagers, whose rights were far more tenuous than those of the small customary tenants, would have been widely tolerated.

The structure of rural society in north Westmorland in the later eighteenth century: the 1787 census

A window on the social structure of villages in north Westmorland at the start of the most rapid period of social and economic change is provided by the 1787 'census' of Westmorland.[31] Though variable in quality and detail between different townships, it allows some conclusions to be drawn regarding the social and occupational structure of households and communities, particularly the numbers of wage labourers in the population compared with living-in servants and adult members of farming families. Table 5.1 presents data for nine townships for which detailed information on household structure as well as occupations is available. They range from lowland communities like Colby to upland ones such as Stainmore. There were substantially fewer labourers than living-in farm servants. The former accounted for only 9 per cent of the male farm labour force

29. Winchester, *Harvest of the Hills*, pp. 79–81.
30. Whyte, *Transforming Fell and Valley*, pp. 34–5.
31. L. Ashcroft, *Vital Statistics: the Westmorland 'Census' of 1787* (Kendal, 1992).

Table 5.1 Breakdown of agricultural workforce for nine Westmorland townships

| Township | Male workers | | | | | | Female workers | | | |
| | Family | | Servants | | Labourers | | Family | | Servants | |
	No.	%	No.	%	No.	%	No.	%	No.	%
Colby	19	70%	6	22%	2	8%	14	52%	13	48%
Hilton	26	84%	5	16%	0	0%	32	94%	2	6%
Murton	22	69%	8	25%	2	6%	16	80%	4	20%
Stainmore	126	82%	8	6%	18	12%	154	88%	21	22%
Kaber	30	67%	5	11%	10	22%	29	85%	5	15%
Milburn	46	82%	7	13%	3	5%	39	78%	11	22%
Knock	27	96%	1	4%	0	0%	19	95%	1	5%
Burton	12	80%	3	20%	0	0%	12	92%	1	8%
Newbiggin	9	47%	7	37%	3	16%	8	53%	7	47%
Total	317	78%	51	13%	38	9%	323	83%	65	17%

Source: 1787 census.

while 78 per cent came from members of farming families. In fact there were probably even fewer agricultural labourers than this suggests because two of the nine townships, Kaber and Stainmore, contained quarries, coal mines and lead mines: some of the people listed as labourers there were probably industrial workers.

Female farm servants, while more common than their male counterparts, were heavily outnumbered by the wives, adult daughters and other female relatives of farmers. For another, larger group of townships it is possible to relate numbers of hired workers (male and female living-in servants and wage labourers) to the number of holdings. Table 5.2 indicates that many farms were worked by family labour alone. In fourteen communities with 288 farms only forty-one labourers were listed. The census confirms then that there were relatively few cottagers or landless labourers and widespread access to land. The use of family labour was normal on small farms and many small farmers were also part-time tradesmen.

It is possible to discover more about the dual occupations of Westmorland villagers at this time by matching data in the 1787 census with near-contemporary enclosure awards. In townships like Brampton and Temple Sowerby it is clear that a number of people listed as, for example, carpenters, tanners and weavers in the census occupied enough property to qualify for substantial allotments of up to 14 acres and were really husbandmen with part-time trades.[32]

Parliamentary enclosure and the self-contained village community

Parliamentary enclosure has been seen as a process which profoundly altered the social cohesion of the eighteenth-century English village. It has been claimed that it demolished surviving elements of a peasantry, creating in its place a tripartite

32. Cumbria Record Office (henceforth CRO) (Kendal), WQR/I/12, 87.

Table 5.2 Numbers of hired workers in relation to holdings in fourteen Westmorland townships

Township	Holdings	Male servants	Labourers	Female servants
Bolton	26	8	7	5
Clifton	20	2	6	8
Crosby Ravensworth	29	11	4	10
Great Strickland	20	6	1	5
Hackthorpe	13	4	3	3
Hartsop	26	2	4	7
King's Meaburn	25	9	0	8
Martindale	20	13	0	10
Maulds Meaburn	34	13	4	11
Morland	14	4	3	3
Newby	20	6	3	7
Reagill	16	8	0	9
Rosgill	16	1	3	8
Sockbridge	9	6	3	5
Total	288	99	41	93

Source: 1787 census.

rural society of landowners, tenant farmers and labourers. In the process the traditional character of village communities was considered to have been irrevocably altered.[33] The background to parliamentary enclosure in Cumbria was different from that of other parts of England, first because almost all the land involved was common pasture and waste, and second because of the distinctiveness of customary tenures which gave even the smallest holders an accepted right to an allotment and a say in the decision regarding whether to enclose.

Was the impact of enclosure on rural communities similar in Cumbria?

By the 1760s the pressures on the commons outlined above were sufficiently widespread and serious to generate increasing demand for their enclosure under parliamentary act. The enclosure of smaller areas of common was already being undertaken by private agreement.[34] The use of a parliamentary act facilitated the enclosure of larger commons with higher numbers of landholders. Two groups in Cumbrian society undoubtedly benefited from enclosure. Manorial lords received

33. The classic study outlining the socialist view of the impact of parliamentary enclosure is J. L. and B. Hammond, *The Village Labourer* (London, 1911). For recent surveys of the long-running debate on parliamentary enclosure and its social impacts see Allen, *Enclosure and the Yeoman*; Neeson, *Commoners*; and G. E. Mingay, *Parliamentary Enclosure in England: an Introduction to its Causes, Incidence and Impact* (London, 1997).
34. I. D. Whyte, 'Patterns of parliamentary enclosure of waste land in Cumbria: a case study from north Westmorland', *Landscape Hist.* 22 (2000), p. 84.

shares of the enclosed lands, as much as a twelfth, in return for relinquishing their rights to the soil (though they usually retained the mineral rights). This share often amounted to an allotment of 100 acres or so, sufficient to create a substantial new leasehold farm. The larger freeholders and customary tenants, embracing agrarian capitalism, received substantial allotments to add to their existing holdings in lieu of their customary rights, particularly to grazing, which in many cases were probably of limited value anyway. The advantages of enclosure for a third group, the smaller customary tenants, are less clear. They also received allotments in lieu of their use-rights on the commons which are often likely to have been of limited value because of the pressures on access discussed above. Under such circumstances they appear to have seen some advantages in having their commons enclosed and receiving shares which they could manage individually, particularly as many commons in areas like the Eden valley were at relatively low altitudes on reasonably fertile soils, and so were suitable for cultivation.[35] Effectively, they were fighting a defensive rearguard action to maintain the status quo of peasant production and society. They seem to have accepted enclosure reluctantly as the only way in which they would get anything of value out of the commons.[36]

The final group in Cumbrian society, the landless labourers and cottagers, are least likely to have benefited directly from enclosure and in some cases may have lost use-rights to the commons without adequate compensation. However, on many commons their rights to graze animals had already been curtailed. Any theoretical rights to cut distant supplies of peat on the commons for fuel may have meant very little to them in practice if they did not have the use of a horse and cart to transport it from a distant peat moss.[37] On the other hand the short-term increase in the demand for labour for creating the new enclosed landscape, and the longer-term labour requirements of a more intensified farming system, may have provided a more tangible economic benefit at a time when rural population was growing and the labouring element increasing.

It has been claimed that the lack of opposition to parliamentary enclosure in Cumbria demonstrates that it was not detrimental to small proprietors. Where opposition, in the form of counter-petitions, did occur it was usually on local, specific issues rather than on the idea of enclosure per se.[38] In addition, where lists of proprietors supporting or opposing an enclosure bill have survived only a

35. Searle, 'Customary economy', p. 147.
36. Searle, 'Parliamentary enclosure movement', p. 263.
37. J. Chapman, 'Parliamentary enclosure in the uplands', in I. D. Whyte and A. J. L. Winchester, eds, *Landscape, Environment and Society in Upland Britain* (Society for Landscape Studies Special Publication, 2, 2005), p. 81.
38. Searle, 'Customary economy', p. 147.

small minority stood out against the change.[39] However, we should be cautious about making assumptions about the motives involved in small customary tenants accepting enclosure. Christopher Dobson, the land steward for the Musgrave estates near Penrith, recorded in 1770 that the tenants of Bleatarn were pushing for the enclosure of their common. This might be taken as demonstrating their enthusiasm for enclosure had not Dobson gone on to remark that their reason was that the neighbouring manor of Ormside had just been bought by the Earl of Thanet who, it was expected, would seek to enclose Ormside common immediately. If that happened, the commoners of Bleatarn expected that their own common would come under severe grazing pressure. They were reluctantly voting for enclosure as the only way to protect their interests.[40]

Even so, it can be demonstrated in other instances that the initiative to enclose arose from the customary tenants rather than the larger freeholders and manorial lords. Dobson, in his correspondence, listed four such cases on a single estate between 1770 and 1772, as well as Bleatarn, noted above.[41] On the other hand if all the customary tenants decided to oppose enclosure they could constitute a formidable block of opinion. In 1767 the customary tenants of Ravenstonedale drew up a petition against an attempt by Sir James Lowther (whose nickname 'Jimmy Grasp-All' speaks volumes) to enclose the commons in the manor. The petition succeeded and the commons remain unenclosed today.[42] More generally, the fact that parliamentary enclosure was not automatically accepted as advantageous is shown by the survival today of extensive unenclosed commons. In Westmorland, while 21 per cent of the area of the county was enclosed under parliamentary act, 27 per cent was never enclosed at all. The extensive commons of the central Lake District in particular are a testimony to the fact that some upland terrain was too rugged for enclosure to be viable.[43]

Notices in newspapers also indicate that the process of initiating enclosure did not always run smoothly. There are many instances where notices indicating an intention to apply to Parliament for permission to introduce a bill were repeated several times before an act was eventually obtained, suggesting if not opposition then at least less than total conviction. The *Westmorland Advertiser* and *Kendal Chronicle* carried a dozen such notices between 1812 and 1819 for manors where

39. For example, CRO (Kendal), WQR/I Miscellaneous enclosure papers, Dufton and Reagill; Lancashire Record Office (Barrow), BD/17/8 Broughton in Furness.
40. See the correspondence between Christopher Dobson and Sir Philip Musgrave on the Edenhall estate over Bleatarn common, CRO (Kendal), WD/CAT/Mus A2173. Letters 10/12/1770, 12/1/1771.
41. CRO (Kendal), WD/CAT/Mus A2173.
42. CRO (Kendal), WQR/I/72.
43. W. G. Hoskins and L. D. Stamp, *The Common Lands of England and Wales* (London, 1963), Appendix A.

enclosure was very belated or never occurred at all.[44] It is likely that the tenants on most Cumbrian manors must have considered the desirability of parliamentary enclosure at some point between the 1760s and 1860s – in some cases demonstrably more than once – but in many cases either the existing management of the commons was acceptable or the costs and other disadvantages of enclosure were thought to outweigh the benefits and no application was made to Parliament. This again argues for a good deal of community solidarity.

If the customary tenants on many manors seem to have had some real choice regarding enclosure, how did they fare when it actually occurred? The first point to make is that even the smallest customary tenants had their rights accepted and were awarded allotments. Enclosure awards sometimes made special provisions for smallholders, not all of whom necessarily had common rights. Did allotment holders, especially the smaller ones, dispose of their newly awarded land to their wealthier neighbours rather than face the cost of ring-fencing and improving it? First let us consider the costs of parliamentary enclosure in the Cumbrian uplands. Cumbrian enclosure commissioners were able to reduce the public costs of enclosure by selling off portions of the commons to raise cash. The public costs of enclosure may not have been as high then for small proprietors as in southern areas. However, preliminary evidence suggests that the private costs of enclosure may have been greater in Cumbria than in lowland England due to the expenses of improving what was often marginal land. In Great Ormside in 1772 the award specified that everyone occupying a house and land whose property was too modest to be charged land tax, and those whose land tax assessment was under 4s., should be entitled to receive allotments of up to 5 acres.[45] Five of the twenty-three people awarded allotments seem to have fallen into this category. Special measures were also used in some awards to reduce the costs of fencing small allotments. At Burton in Kendal, the allotments of groups of smallholders were amalgamated to form areas of shared stinted pasture, with a substantial reduction in the costs of ring-fencing.[46]

One or two instances do occur where small commons, such as Yanwath, were enclosed at a relatively high cost per acre, to the undoubted disadvantage of small customary tenants, forcing them to sell their allotments to their more prosperous neighbours in circumstances which resemble the classic Marxist model of the Hammonds.[47] It is also clear that some large proprietors – notably the earls of Lowther and Thanet – used enclosure as an opportunity to acquire additional land

44. *Westmorland Advertiser* and *Kendal Herald*, Microfilm, Kendal Library.
45. CRO (Kendal), WQR/I/72.
46. CRO (Kendal), WQR/I/19.
47. Searle, 'Parliamentary enclosure movement', pp. 257–8.

by buying up the allotments of customary tenants. Ongoing research by the author into the land tax lists for Westmorland should shed more light on the degree of continuity of occupation, or otherwise, by small proprietors that occurred following enclosure. However, a study of the awards shows that some proprietors did sell their allotments before the awards were drawn up. The sale of allotments in this way are mentioned in 36 per cent of Westmorland awards, less than the 50 per cent recorded by Martin for Warwickshire but comparable to the 41 per cent in Turner's study of Buckinghamshire.[48] However, sales of allotments amounted to only 3.4 per cent of the total area of land enclosed. While those who sold their allotments were predominantly smallholders, that is not to say that most smallholders sold out. If smallholders are defined as property holders receiving less than 5 acres as allotments, only 21 per cent of smallholders in manors where enclosure occurred sold out. Some of them were demonstrably part-time tradesmen who may have been keen to raise capital for investment elsewhere. In other cases allotments were sold by widows, heirs and trustees of the original owners, possibly in conjunction with the disposal or division of the main holding.

Allotment holders could also have sold their allotments after the enclosure awards had been drawn up and this is harder to identify from the sources. It undoubtedly happened in some instances at least. At Great Ormside, where the award was drawn up in 1772, the earl of Thanet bought the allotments of nine out of twenty-one proprietors between 1773 and 1775, their lands amounting to 28 per cent of the common after the deduction of the manorial and tithe shares.[49]

So parliamentary enclosure affected Cumbrian village communities by encouraging a widening split in rural society between the larger and smaller customary tenants and by causing some reductions in the numbers of smaller proprietors. However, the scale of change in most communities studied appears to have been modest compared with parts of lowland England. Smallholders were not driven out wholesale, encouraging a continuity of tradition. By increasing the sizes of the holdings of many smaller proprietors parliamentary enclosure may indeed have helped to promote continuity in Cumbrian village society through the later eighteenth century into the nineteenth, with changes operating slowly and progressively rather than suddenly.

48. J. M. Martin, 'The parliamentary enclosure movement and rural society in Warwickshire', *Agric. Hist. Rev.* 15 (1967), pp. 19–39; M. Turner, 'The cost of parliamentary enclosure in Buckinghamshire', *Agric. Hist. Rev.* 21 (1973), pp. 35–46.
49. CRO (Kendal), WD/Hoth/Box 23 accounts 1773–75.

Change and crisis in Cumbrian village society: the Napoleonic Wars and their aftermath

The first burst of parliamentary enclosure in Cumbria, as in lowland England, occurred in the 1760s and 1770s. Enclosure peaked during and immediately after the Napoleonic Wars. As parliamentary enclosure became more frequent, however, it also became more contentious. Most of the enclosure processes from the 1770s were completed within a year or two of the act being passed. From the 1790s, however, the period between act and award lengthened so that it sometimes took a decade or more to complete an enclosure. Some of the delays may have been due to the fact that the commons enclosed at this time were often larger than in the 1770s with more claims of common rights to evaluate. Moreover, boundary disputes between adjacent commons and complex claims of rights related to the widespread practice of intercommoning added substantially to delays in many cases.[50] This occurred to such an extent in Cumbria that one landowner claimed that this was the most difficult part of England in which to carry out enclosure.[51]

At this period rural society faced a range of pressures. The first of these was the demand for increased output of cereals which led to the ploughing up of much newly enclosed common, and the conversion of Cumberland and Westmorland, albeit temporarily, from counties which were net importers of grain to net exporters.[52] This must have placed a strain on labour supplies, yet where detailed records have survived of the people who were employed in fencing, road building and land improvement they seem to have been predominantly local people rather than itinerant gangs of outsiders, again emphasising the self-contained character of the labour force.[53]

During the war years, when grain prices rose to near-famine levels, it may have seemed that no farmer, however small, could fail to make a profit. From the less certain years of the 1820s and 1830s, farmers looked back wistfully to what they called the 'Bonneypart' (Bonaparte) time.[54] The pressure to improve newly enclosed land encouraged many small proprietors to borrow money to finance the cost of ring-fencing and land improvement. They also incurred debts in rebuilding and extending their outbuildings and farmhouses.[55] After 1815, however, prices dropped sharply while loans still had to be repaid. In addition wartime pressures

---

50. A. J. L. Winchester, 'Dividing lines in a moorland landscape: territorial boundaries in upland England', *Landscapes* 1 (2000), pp. 16–32.
51. Searle, 'Parliamentary enclosure movement', p. 253.
52. Whyte, *Transforming Fell and Valley*, pp. 26–7.
53. K. D. M. Snell, *Annals of the Labouring Poor* (Cambridge, 1985), pp. 182–6.
54. C. Webster, 'The farming of Westmorland', *Jnl Roy. Ag. Soc. Eng.* 2nd ser. 4 (1868) p. 7.
55. House of Commons, Select Committee on Enclosure, 1833 Vol. V, pp. 303–26.

and profits had encouraged over-cultivation of newly enclosed land with successive crops of cereals, short-term profit outweighing long-term sustainability. Many of the hastily ploughed allotments had to be left to revert to rough pasture and many of their cultivators went bankrupt in the 1820s and 1830s producing what was described as the biggest shake-up in Cumbrian landownership in living memory.[56] The fate of these farmers, recorded in bankruptcy sales in local newspapers, has yet to find its historian. The period from the 1790s to the 1820s appears then to have been marked by greater change in Cumbrian village communities as some smaller proprietors sold their allotments to their larger neighbours. These in turn sometimes 'built themselves out of doors', as one contemporary writer wryly commented, by over-investment in farm improvements using borrowed capital.[57]

Nevertheless, the expansion in the area of improved land, and in some cases the creation of new farms, increased the demand for labour as did associated work in quarrying, lime burning, coal mining and carting. This tended to support traditional village communities rather than undermine them, and may have checked the outflow of labour from rural areas. Farmsteads were not removed out of the villages with enclosure, as happened in areas like the East Riding, because the allotments of former common were normally placed as close to existing holdings as possible.[58] Relatively few new farms were created, and these were mainly on manorial and church allotments.

Mid-nineteenth century enclosure and the shift to commercial livestock rearing

A third burst of parliamentary enclosure took place in the mid-nineteenth century following the 1845 General Enclosure Act which reduced administrative costs significantly.[59] The stimulus to enclose at this period was the expansion of commercial livestock farming as the improvement of communications, particularly the spread of the railway network, put Cumbrian farmers more closely in touch with markets in south Lancashire, Tyneside and even London.[60] In north Westmorland the impact of the railways was striking with the area between the

---

56. Ibid., p. 307.
57. W. Dickinson, 'On the farming of Cumberland', *Jnl. Roy. Ag. Soc. Eng.* 13 (1852), p. 277.
58. W. E. Tate and M. Turner, *A Domesday of English Enclosure Awards* (Reading, 1978), pp. 31–2.
59. This claim is supported by the census of 1821 in which it was specifically stated for the Cumberland parishes of Edenhall, Isell and Great Salkeld that the rise in population since 1811 had been due to enclosure, Parliamentary Papers, *Census of Britain* Vol. VII, pp. 370–83.
60. M. E. Shepherd, 'The small owner in Cumbria c. 1840–1900: a case study from the upper Eden valley,' *Northern Hist.* 35 (1999), pp. 161–84.

Figure 5.2 Maulds Meaburn, Westmorland. Encroachments on the village green have provided accommodation for some cottagers (Photograph by Ian Whyte)

Lancaster–Carlisle Railway, opened in 1846, and the branch line from Tebay over Stainmore to County Durham, opened in 1862, precipitating a surge of enclosure. The growing dependence of Cumbrian farmers on the long-distance trade in livestock, evident from the mid-eighteenth century but reinforced now by the railways, paradoxically encouraged the continuation of self-sufficient farms and communities which still retained an element of traditional peasant society.

The enclosure awards from this period are more detailed than for earlier times and provide more information on the owners of land which can be compared with the 1851 census enumerators' books. The awards often specify the property on which successful claims of common right were based and it is clear that small proprietors continued to flourish in most of the communities concerned. People receiving allotments are listed in the census with dual occupations such as 'bobbin turner and farmer' or 'carpenter and farmer'. Others designated simply as carpenters or stonemasons also received allotments and clearly had enough property to qualify as commoners. Some people receiving allotments held small areas of arable or enclosed pasture but no dwelling, the land perhaps being outliers of main holdings located in neighbouring townships. Others, however, were clearly cottagers with no more than a garden plot or sometimes an orchard. In Maulds Meaburn in 1855 eight of the thirty-three allotment holders were definitely cottagers.[61] (See Figure 5.2.)

61.   CRO (Kendal), WQR/I 64.

Figure 5.3 Crosby Garret, Westmorland. Most of the common of Crosby Garret was never enclosed, but farmers benefited from the coming of the railway in the 1860s, which encouraged a switch to more commercial livestock farming (Photograph by Ian Whyte)

Large and small proprietors in the mid-nineteenth century received allotments which represented substantial additions to existing holdings, as is shown in Table 5.3, causing an upward drift in farm sizes which may have helped to increase their viability. Again some smaller landholders disposed of their allotments before enclosure but not to an extent which is likely to have caused major changes in the structure of village society. Most of the land sold by enclosure commissioners and allotment holders at this time went to local people rather than outsiders and relatively little of it was sold to large proprietors. This suggests that elements of the self-contained village persisted in the area until at least the mid-nineteenth century. Some enclosure commissioners appear to have been particularly keen to sell land in small parcels to men of modest means. In villages like Bolton and Crosby Garret the commissioners auctioned land in as many as twenty small parcels to buyers who were often designated as 'yeomen' but who also included basket-makers, brewers, labourers and stonemasons.[62] (See Figure 5.3.) Some parcels of land were bought by people who either held land on leasehold or who previously had no land at all.

62. CRO (Kendal), WQR/I 10 & 22.

Table 5.3 Average percentage increase in holding size after parliamentary enclosure

Enclosure	Date of award	Average % increase in holding size
Asby Mask	1855	96
Asby Winderwath	1874	65
Colby	1854	28
Grayrigg	1868	75
Great Musgrave	1859	59
Hillbeck	1859	136
Kirkby Stephen	1855	85
Lambrigg	1886	37
Little Musgrave	1853	41
Newbiggin	1850	55
Maulds Meaburn	1858	37
Smardale	1849	135
Waitby	1855	72

Source: enclosure awards.

Conclusion

It must first be acknowledged that Cumbrian village communities did change between the 1760s and the 1860s. Dual occupations and rural industry declined in many areas. As communications improved rural communities concentrated more on livestock rearing for the growing industrial towns. The proportion of small proprietors also seems to have declined, though not drastically and this occurred in villages which did not experience parliamentary enclosure as well as ones which did. The basic structure of Cumbrian village society, with its emphasis on small family farms, continued into the late nineteenth and even the twentieth century. This society, paradoxically, was sustained by the long-distance trade in livestock and their products, the hungry population of Manchester and its satellites helping to maintain elements of a traditional peasant society less than a hundred miles away. Cumbrian peasant farmers were so resilient because they were prepared to work hard and accept modest profits, especially by reducing costs through their use of family labour. The lifestyle of such farmers has been seen by some commentators as doggedly independent, but by others as a form of slavery. This study has shown that while numbers of small proprietors may have declined in Cumbria as a result of the economic and social changes of the late eighteenth and early nineteenth centuries they were not, as a class, squeezed off the land and converted into dependent wage labourers on the scale that has been suggested for lowland England. In particular, parliamentary enclosure did not have the destabilising effect on rural society that occurred in parts of southern and midland England. The numbers of small owner-occupiers may have been reduced but their survival as a class helped Cumbrian rural communities to retain something of their self-sufficient character until well into the later nineteenth century.[63]

It must be acknowledged that some of the arguments presented here are speculative and require more detailed research to substantiate them. In particular, detailed comparison of the land tax lists with enclosure awards should provide a better picture of the changes in landownership during the crucial years of the late eighteenth and early nineteenth centuries. We do not know enough about the scale of local variation in communities, nor do we know enough about influences such as the management policies of the larger estates. While a good deal of work has been undertaken into aspects of Cumbrian society in the seventeenth and early eighteenth centuries, and some has recently been done for the later nineteenth century there is ample scope for more detailed community studies relating to the period of most rapid change in between. Such studies should help to clarify the extent to, and the ways in which, continuity of peasant traditions was maintained in Cumbria.

63. M. E. Shepherd, *From Hellgill to Bridge End: Aspects of Economic and Social Change in the Upper Eden Valley, 1840–95* (Hatfield, 2003).

6

The rise of industrial society and the end of the self-contained village, 1760–1900?

DAVID BROWN

Many discussions of the self-contained village – here interpreted as a unit of settlement including hamlets and squatter colonies as well as nucleated villages – belong to the period before 1760.[1] While there is much merit in the idea of the long eighteenth century, particularly in terms of the pace of economic growth and development of certain service industries like retailing, the years around 1760 mark a watershed in important ways. In the dramatic demographic and social changes described as the 'Industrial Revolution' (with rapid urbanisation, the transformation of agricultural production, employment patterns and transport developments)[2] village independence is tacitly assumed to have been eroded in terms of demography, economy, administration and culture.[3]

To establish the accuracy of this view, it is necessary to establish criteria for assessing the independence of villages; these yardsticks then need to be applied to assess to what extent the rise of industrial society reduced village self-containedness and whether this occurred consistently throughout Britain. The latter requires a 'local' approach through which patterns emerge to explain any uneven application of the trend towards integration. There had always been different types of rural settlement, most obviously villages and hamlets; but industrialisation spawned new kinds of settlement like squatter colonies, industrial villages, textile colonies and model villages. 'Urban villages' were even found in growing towns due to residential segregation. As this apparent oxymoron illustrates, a clear typology cannot be easily established. Indeed the point when a village becomes urbanised in industrial areas is often debatable. Sometimes, the law provides clarification. Bilston (Staffordshire) 'one of the largest villages in England', secured a local act in 1824 to establish a market and a

1. I would like to express my thanks to Christopher Dyer for his helpful advice in editing this article.
2. N. F. R. Crafts, *British Economic Growth during the Industrial Revolution* (Oxford, 1985).
3. *Times*, 17 January 1924, p. 13 col. d, review of Lord Ernle, *Our English Villages*, *Quarterly Review* 1924; W. E. Tate, *The English Village Community and the Enclosure Movements* (London, 1967), p. 175.

town hall.[4] More common were improvement acts or the decision to adopt the General Lighting and Watching act of 1834 which *de facto* established a form of urban authority.[5] Outside these cases, problems of definition occur; as Court famously commented of the Black Country, the growing villages often retained much of the rural alongside the urban before they could be christened towns. Additionally an 'industrial village' like Darlaston or a 'manufacturing hamlet' like Smethwick, both in Staffordshire, had populations in excess of 8,000 in 1851, whereas Longnor, a market town in the same county, only had 561 inhabitants.[6]

There are several overlapping indicators by which a village's 'self-containedness' can be assessed. One is its formal legal independence, as the wide powers of the medieval manorial court were gradually eroded by the royal courts, quarter sessions and statute law. Nevertheless, the interpretation and enforcement of the law remained in the hands of the local landowners in 1760. While parishioners could appeal to the quarter sessions, the ability of most of them to afford legal representation and to gain access, without the support and sympathy of a local magistrate, is questionable.

A second indicator is demographic separation, which can be measured to an extent by levels of out-marriage or of immigration and emigration. Certainly the level of migration in early modern Britain was far greater than was previously believed.[7] The third yardstick – the economic autonomy of the village – was apparently undermined more by the advent of industrial society than any other factor. While village economies were never hermetically sealed (see pp. 23–4), and both rural industries and itinerant retailing had developed in the early modern age, commercial intercourse was limited and often conducted through the conduit of intermediaries like chapmen and carriers. From the eighteenth century, improving transport and the progress of consumerism brought villages increasingly within a regional and national economy.

A fourth criterion is the most intangible but is closely related to the others – the cultural self-containedness of the village. While the hardest to demonstrate quantifiably, this measure is probably the most important. It will be dealt with *pari passu* with the other three criteria, and in the discussion about the model villages which emerged in this period.

As is already clear, the independence and separation of villages had already been eroded by 1760, but changes connected with the industrialisation of society

4.   5 Geo. IV, c. li.
5.   3 & 4 William IV, c. 90, Lighting and Watching Act.
6.   W. H. B. Court, *The Rise of the Midland Industries* (Oxford, 1938), pp. 21–2; W. White, *Staffordshire* (Sheffield, 1851), pp. 598, 704 and 743.
7.   D. Brown, 'An Honest, Industrious and Useful Description of People': *Itinerant Retailing and its Role in the Economy 1600–1900* (forthcoming, London, 2006), Chapter 4.

thereafter accelerated the process according to all of the four criteria. First, the process brought in its wake limitations on the self-government of villages. As industrial society developed, so too did the powers of central authority. It is a paradox that as free market capitalism blossomed, a laissez-faire approach to society's management wilted. The new philosophy of industrial society – utilitarianism – despite the paternalist reaction of many of the slowly declining aristocracy, created a homogenising culture which reduced local autonomy. Concerns about the separate morality and culture of politically and socially independent settlements prompted legislation tightening central control. The 1834 Poor Law sought to standardise the management of pauperism; the anomalous jurisdictions of extra-parochials and closed parishes were ended by legislation like the Union Chargeability Act of 1865. Poor law unions created administrative connections beyond the parish and brought 'open' parishes under the influence of local landowners. Apart from new local and national administrative bodies, new institutions like the county police, universal after 1856, and county councils after 1888, reduced parochial liberty.

The paternalist reaction to industrialisation, rapid population growth and perceived independent-mindedness of the poor also reduced the legal and consequently the cultural self-containedness of villages. Voluntary local initiative, sometimes assisted by permissive legislation and funds from general taxation to match local fund raising, produced a growing number of institutions which tended to homogenise village culture. For example, acts of 1819 and 1831 facilitated the purchase of garden grounds in both towns and villages; religious education after 1833 increased, based on local fund raising and increasing central subventions. Savings clubs and agricultural societies with prizes for farmers and cottagers were also established by local landowners in many villages. An example of how concerns about the culture of the poor provoked paternal intervention was the attempted formation of a village club association in Suffolk in 1876, after the bitter agricultural labourers' strike. Such clubs would provide books, lecturers, provident societies and savings banks, and they would sell beer more responsibly than pubs. In this spirit, Captain Polhill-Turner in Bedfordshire welcomed 'the happy bond and unionism they had at Renhold, unionism between landlord and tenant, master and men.'[8]

Of all institutions, the most energetic efforts were made to provide an Anglican presence in rural communities, typically churches in settlements away from the parish centre. Thus in 1837 land and money were offered for an 'episcopal chapel'

8.   59 George III, c. 12; 1 and 2 William IV, c. 42; *Times*, 23 October 1876, p. 4 col. d, 'A village club association'; N. Agar, *The Bedfordshire Farm Worker in the Nineteenth Century* (Bedfordshire Hist. Record Soc., 60, 1981), p. 195.

in the tithing of Chittoe, 7 miles from the parish church at Bishops Cannings in Wiltshire.[9] Research in rural parts of highly industrialised Staffordshire reinforces this view where the rate of church building in Pirehill South Hundred exceeded that of the county as a whole. In 1851, 40.7 per cent of Staffordshire's churches had been built in the previous half-century; however while central encouragement was given to church extension in industrial villages and suburbs, there was also much activity in rural settlements. In the twenty-two parishes of Pirehill South Hundred, thirteen had a new place of worship, nine had their churches rebuilt, eight parsonages and sixteen schools were built during the previous half-century.[10] This effort had complicated consequences for the self-containedness of settlements. Both hamlets with new churches or villages with rebuilt churches now had a greater Anglican presence, which reduced the need to look outside for their spiritual or educational needs. Conversely, the independent peasant culture of the village was threatened by resident clerics and schoolmasters who encouraged, exhorted and indoctrinated towards an alternative world view. In Nomans Heath, an extra-parochial district at the meeting of three counties including Staffordshire, the arrival of a school, a church and a resident cleric, and its parochialisation, together with its inclusion within a poor law union, addressed the falsely perceived criminality of the settlement.[11] The paranoia of the landed elite about isolated settlements in particular is indicated by this astonishing claim by the son of a nearby rural rector about a squatter colony in the Black Country:

> The Lye Waste boasted that coroner's inquests on infanticide were unknown in its area. There was some truth in the taunt, despite the notorious immorality of the district, but the solution was simple. Most Lye Wasters kept pigs; if there chanced to be a superfluous baby the family pig was kept on short commons for a day or so. Then the infant (somehow) 'fell' into the sty! ... and in half an hour no coroner could have found, any remains to sit upon.[12]

Equally, when an apparently insane Primitive Methodist labourer from a Bedfordshire village murdered an old woman in 1853, the newspaper report blamed the settlement's remoteness and consequent nonconformity. 'Heath and Reach is a long and lonely village; a good proportion of its inhabitants may fairly be described as unusually ignorant, and wild and fanatic religious opinions

9.   *Times*, 26 October 1837, p. 2 col. d.
10. W. White, *History, Gazetteer and Directory of Staffordshire* (Sheffield, 1851).
11. D. Brown, 'The relationship between local elites and central government: the Victorian attempts to "reform" Nomans Heath', *Jnl of Victorian Culture* 2 (1997), pp. 42–70; A. Brundage, *The Making of the New Poor Law* (New Brunswick, NJ, 1978), pp. 181–4.
12. W. B. Woodgate, *Reminiscences of a Sportsman* (London, 1907), p. 40.

distinguish many of them.' Fortunately one of the new county police was on hand next door to arrest the labourer.[13]

Similar fears, often unjustified, were entertained about isolated settlements, especially squatter colonies.[14] For example Dunkirk, an extra-parochial in Kent, received similar paternal treatment to Nomans Heath after it was blamed for the last labourers' revolt in 1830, though the accusation was not justified as most of the rioters came from an adjoining parish. Isolated or squatter settlements had their own culture but this often posed no real threat to society; the inhabitants were often industrious petty capitalists and farmers and as law abiding as their parochial neighbours.[15] However the alleged danger of separateness was often a pretext for reducing the administrative independence of places sometimes isolated by culture rather than physical distance. Thus, according to a Spitalfields lace manufacturer around 1795, the village of Haggerstone in Shoreditch, only two miles from St Paul's in London, was inhabited by

> brick makers ... the very lowest class of society ... no man or woman towards dark will walk that way towards Hackney ... if a thief was pursued and ran to Haggerstone, no constable or runner would go beyond a certain line; it has been called 'The City of Refuge'.

However its 'improved state' by 1815 was attributed to the impact of volunteers at Sunday Schools. Thereafter a new church in 1827 continued Haggerstone's 'improvement' – but even the district's critics acknowledged that it was populated by workers rather than just criminals and beggars.[16]

Apart from these institutional and administrative changes, demographic change also affected the self-containedness of villages. Migration, ever present, increased during the long eighteenth century. One estimate suggests around 70 per cent of people migrated in the eighteenth century, but the character of the movements varied according to local circumstances.[17] For example in arable

13. *Times*, 28 November 1853, p. 9 col. f.
14. See summary of the Board of Agriculture Reports on squatters in Tate, *English Village Community*, pp. 164–5.
15. B. Reay, *The Last Rising of the Agricultural Labourers: Rural Life and Protest in Nineteenth-Century England* (Oxford, 1990); D. Brown, 'The variety of motives for parliamentary enclosure: the example of the Cannock Chase area 1773–1867', *Midland Hist.* 19 (1994), pp. 105–27; D. Brown, ' "Persons of infamous character" or "an honest, industrious and useful description of people"? The textile pedlars of Alstonfield and the role of peddling in industrialization', *Textile Hist.* 31 (2000), pp. 1–25.
16. *Times*, 17 August 1815, p. 2 col. b, 'Mendicity'; 21 August 1815, p. 2 col. d; and 19 July 1827, p. 3 col. b; *The National Gazetteer* (1868), sub Shoreditch; W. Hale, *Letter to Sam. Whitbread ... Observations on Poor of Spitalfields* (London, 1806), p. 26.
17. P. Clark, 'Migration in England during the late seventeenth and early eighteenth centuries', *Past and Present* 85 (1979), pp. 57–90; K. D. M. Snell, 'Parish registration and the study of labour mobility', *Local Population Studies* 32 (1984), pp. 29–43.

areas, seasonal migration was hardly known before 1640 but by 1800 it had become common, at a time of greater efficiency, specialisation and increased productivity. The rate of acceleration increased after 1760 and impacted on the separateness of villages as these temporary inhabitants limited the permanent core of labour.[18] In industrial villages like Calverley in the West Riding textile district, there was a semi-permanent core of residents, largely the independent weavers, but immigrants (typically from 1800 to the spinning mills), even with local connections, often failed to settle and moved on, if only for short distances. Industrial workers in Yorkshire moved further afield but only between manufacturing districts within the county.[19] Miners perforce migrated longer distances from declining to developing coalfields and migration from Ireland and parts of Scotland accelerated, aided by cheaper transport by the late nineteenth century.[20] The core population and the newcomers were often mutually antagonistic and sometimes violent; poor arrivals, particularly if associated with a particular place (frequently Ireland), united especially under accusations of criminality and dirtiness. Wherever the newcomers formed communities – ghettoised urban villages like the ubiquitous 'Little Ireland' or mining villages – these tended to be inward-looking because the residents' common cultural background was alien to that of their new surroundings.[21]

Most existing agricultural villages experienced some growth but their surplus population, often lacking local employment opportunities, migrated to find work. This impacted on the villages themselves as migrants were often their fittest and most active members.[22] Although between 1841 and 1901 about half a million in each decade left villages for towns, in earlier times migrants went to existing villages with domestic industries and squatter colonies on convenient

---

18. E. J. T. Collins, 'Migrant labour in British agriculture in the nineteenth century', Econ. Hist. Rev. 2nd ser. 29 (1976), pp. 38–60; J. Thirsk, Alternative Agriculture: a History from the Black Death to the Present Day (Oxford, 1997).

19. S. A. King, 'Calverley und Sowerby. Die Protoindustrielle Entwicklung in zwei Gemeinden Yorkshires, 1660 bis 1830', in W. Mager and D. Ebeling, eds, Proto-industrie in der Region: Europaissche Gewerbelandschaften vom 16. bis 19. Jahrhunderts (Bielefeld, 1997), pp. 221–54; C. Pooley and J. Turnbull, Migration and Mobility in Britain since the Eighteenth Century (London, 1998); B. A. Holderness, 'Personal mobility in some rural parishes of Yorkshire 1777–1822', Yorkshire Arch. Jnl 42 (1972), pp. 444–54; A. G. Crosby, ed., The Family Records of Benjamin Shaw Mechanic of Dent, Dolphinholme and Preston, 1772–1841 (Gloucester, 1991).

20. M. Turner, ed., Kith and Kin: Nidderdale Families, 1500–1750 (Summerbridge, 1995); Shropshire Record Office, 1781/5/5, autobiography of George Jones of Shackerley, p. 56.

21. Times, 2 October 1866, p. 5 col. g; J. Langton, 'People from the pits: the origins of colliers in eighteenth-century southwest Lancashire', in C. Pooley and I. White, eds, Migrants, Emigrants and Immigrants (London, 1991), pp. 106–42.

22. J. Long, 'Rural-urban migration and socioeconomic mobility in Victorian Britain', Jnl of Econ. Hist. 65 (2005), pp. 1–34.

Figure 6.1 Knife grinder, *c.* 1800. Itinerants not only sold goods but also their labour. The original caption added 'there is a picturesque diversity in the various machines travelling about the country', some being carried on the back, others fitted into a small cart (Source: W. Pyne, *The Costume of Great Britain* [London, 1819])

commons.[23] From the mid-seventeenth century these settlements had developed on commons and wastes away from traditional parish centres. Apart from population pressure, there were many factors which led to the emergence of such new settlements. One was geological – the quality of the soil and the usefulness of the underlying rocks and minerals. Another was the presence of extensive commons in areas of low population where freeholders would tolerate some diminution of rough grazing. Divided or confused manorial and parochial jurisdictions encouraged settlement because the lords and overseers were unable to police encroachment effectively. In some cases, proximity to transport routes, suppliers and markets were attractions to settlement. More frequently encountered in the north and west, these squatter settlements depended upon spade husbandry, exploitation of the commons for grazing and fuel, and cultivation of barley and oats. Most squatters also engaged in a wide spectrum of

23.   F. Crouzet, *The Victorian Economy* (London, 1982), p. 93; E. G. Ravenstein, 'The laws of migration', *Jnl. Roy. Statistical Soc.* 48 (1885), pp. 167–227.

Figure 6.2 Rustics, c. 1800. Males and females carried goods either for sale or delivery. Itinerant retailers and those bringing goods provided a source of gossip, news and ideas, linking villages and towns (Source: W. Pyne, *Microcosm* [London, 1806])

alternative economic activity dependent on local factors. Where minerals outcropped or lay near the surface, squatters engaged in mining on their own account or for the manorial lord or his lessee. In Blackborough (Devon) in the Blackdown Hills, whetstones were manufactured. In the vicinity of ironworks, nailers' settlements grew up as in the Black Country. In scrubby commons like Cheslyn Hay on Cannock Chase in Staffordshire, besoms and other basket wares were made for local itinerant sale. These settlements were perceived as having a distinct culture – at Blackborough (Devon), Flash (Staffordshire) and Biddulph Moor (Staffordshire) myths arose that the inhabitants were aliens with their own lifestyle and dialect. (See Figure 6.1.)

The 'Biddle Moor' sellers were believed to have originated from Indian servants who settled there around 1700. They played to the romance of their cultural differences in their sales pitch with their wares spread around a box in a market place. The box was hammered with a stick to punctuate a patter delivered in a quick, shrill and staccato tone, strangling the syllables so that the audience understood little but the price, which suspiciously the sellers ensured was

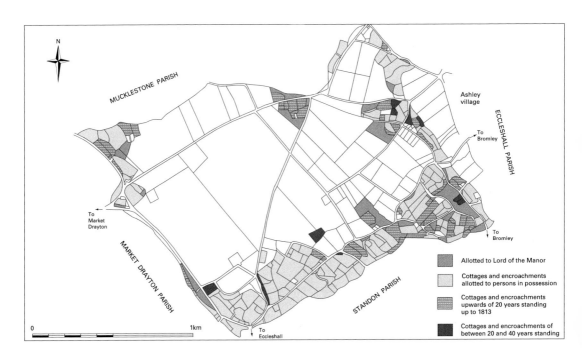

Figure 6.3 Ashley Heath enclosure award map, 1830. On this common on the Staffordshire/Shropshire border many of the encroachments contained cottages. The enclosure was aimed at preventing 'the increase of the poor' and 'the whole commons being inclosed by the cottagers' (Sources: Staffordshire Record Office, Q/RDc80 1830; D240/E/C/1/10/11 and D240/E/C/1/10/8)

sufficiently distinctive for buyers to understand.[24] Biddulph Moor was among a small group of squatter settlements of itinerant retailers who used their moorland encroachments for smallholdings, and perhaps for their horses. Their selling campaigns were often extensive and took several months. For example, the pedlars of Alstonfield in north Staffordshire from 1700 traded first in locally made buttons and then in smallwares from nearby manufacturing districts, which they carried along the newly turnpiked roads to eastern England. These communities were strongly bound, as the itinerants either combined together to obtain stock on credit, or depended upon one of the more successful of their number to provide the capital for their enterprises.[25] (See Figure 6.2.)

Squatter settlements generally were often distant from existing villages and their isolation was perceived as dangerous by the local elite. Squatter colonies were attacked in the 1844 Select Committee on Commons Inclosure as being in 'a world of themselves' whose inhabitants were disinclined to attend the established

24. G. W. Rhead and F. A. Rhead, *Staffordshire Pots and Potters* (London, 1906), pp. 341–5.
25. D. Brown, 'The autobiography of a pedlar: John Lomas of Hollinsclough (1747–1823)', *Midland Hist.* 21 (1996), pp. 156–66.

Table 6.1 The population of Fradswell, Staffordshire, 1666–1901

Year	1666	1801	1811	1821	1831	1841	1851	1861	1871	1881	1891	1901
Population	145	163	246	219	199	237	244	220	209	199	180	166
Houses	29	29	38	–	–	42	45	47	43	43	40	–

Sources: E. Grogan, ed., 'Hearth tax for the hundred of Pirehill for 1666', *Collections for History of Staffordshire* (1921), p. 74 (assuming multiplier of five per household); Census returns 1801–1901.

church. Such settlements were often viewed as centres of criminality despite the fact that many like Heath and Reach (Bedfordshire) were hotbeds of nonconformity, which adopted stricter regimes of self-discipline than those imposed by the Anglican church in the second half of the eighteenth century. Some communities grew so large that whole commons disappeared or very nearly did so under pressure of numbers.[26] For example, the enclosure award for Ashley Heath (Shropshire/Staffordshire) shows the high level of encroachment which had occurred before enclosure (see Figure 6.3).

In such areas, parliamentary enclosure after 1760 was one way of dealing with disorganised settlement and independent individuals; in enclosure acts, a rule of twenty years uninterrupted enjoyment was often adopted in determining ownership of encroachments. A pattern emerges of freeholders instigating perambulations of commons to open encroachments to prevent squatters gaining possession. Eventually they applied to the manorial lord to enclose, rarely to expel the encroachers but to prevent the common's further shrinkage. The lord was usually allotted encroachments of fewer than twenty years' standing which enabled him to convert the 'owners' into tenants. However in some cases, lords used the law to remove inconvenient squatters. Fradswell Heath, a very poor area of cottages about a mile away from Fradswell village in Staffordshire, was considered to be a squatter settlement of low morals. The manorial rights were disputed and the whole village was a chapelry 9 miles away from the parish's centre. Lord Ferrers, whose Chartley Castle estate adjoined the common, bought the manorial rights, obtained an enclosure by act in 1852, and secured the area of the encroachments. Within a decade, the cottages had disappeared and, as Table 6.1 shows, the population and number of houses of Fradswell fell in a county whose population was rising rapidly.[27]

Similarly, the hillside squatter settlement on Little Doward Hill in Ganarew (Herefordshire), overlooking the romantic river Wye, adjoined the park of a wealthy landowner, Richard Blakemore. The overseers were unable to remove the

26. S. C. on Commons Inclosure (P. P. 1844, V), QQ. 4122, 4182–4242; D. Brown, 'Enclosure and improvement: an investigation into the motives for parliamentary enclosure' (unpublished Ph.D. thesis, Wolverhampton, 1992), pp. 96–8 and 231–2.
27. Staffordshire Record Office (hereafter SRO), Q/RDc, Fradswell Heath enclosure award 1856.

Table 6.2 The population of Ganarew, Herefordshire, 1801–41

Year	1801	1811	1821	1831	1841
Population	88	74	118	148	123

Sources: Census returns 1801–41.

encroachments which increased the population and the poor rates and a committee was formed to stop squatting 'either by act of parliament or otherwise.' The Enclosure Act of 1833 even cited this problem as its motivation and it allowed Blakemore to buy nearly all the common to extend his park and reversed the population increase as shown in Table 6.2. The assistant overseer's allowance was reduced 'in consequence of the Inclosure of Doward' and poor rates fell by 30 per cent. Similarly at the Vyne in Hampshire, the inheritance of a Utilitarian landowner in 1826 led to the parish's enclosure, the destruction of a squatter settlement and an assisted emigration scheme, resulting in lower poor rates and falling population. Less drastic cultural engineering was intended by the Tory lord of the manor in the enclosure of Alstonfield in the Staffordshire moorlands in 1834. He hoped it 'will make a vast difference by tending to concentrate and civilise the wild folk who dwell among the hills. The roguish will be brought into light by new roads, opened into the recesses where they have carried on in darkness their bad practices.' In enclosures of many royal forests, squatters were concentrated into villages with new churches to be more easily policed.[28]

Later migrants seemingly preferred an urban slum to a squatter's cottage and the inexorable rise of population in towns challenged the independence of villages.[29] The physical expansion of towns swallowed up some villages and the improvements in transport in the eighteenth and nineteenth centuries brought others increasingly within the urban orbit. Headington Quarry's original existence was to provide stone for Oxford's dreaming spires; although the later squatter settlement retained some of its autonomous character, its restored economic dependence upon Oxford is noteworthy.[30] Settlements adjoining old boroughs like Dorchester, Norwich or Market Drayton were engulfed, and efforts to reform them met with variable success. In other cases, a cluster of industrial villages coalesced into a town; West Bromwich during the first half of the nineteenth

28. Herefordshire Record Office, AC 75/26; Q/Ri/18, Ganarew enclosure award 1835; E. C. Lascelles, *Directory of Herefordshire* (Hereford, 1851), pp. 139–40; Hampshire Record Office, 31 M 57/1072; D. R. Mills, *Lord and Peasant in Nineteenth-Century Britain* (London, 1980), pp. 102, 106 and 129; Derbyshire Record Office, D2375/m/44/1 and D2375/m/40/7–14, Sir George Crewe's Journals 1829–1841; Brown, 'Enclosure and improvement', Table 25 Section 5 and Table 28.
29. D. Feldman, 'Migration', in M. Daunton, ed., *The Cambridge Urban History of Britain III 1840–1950* (Cambridge, 2000), pp. 185 and 189.
30. R. Samuel, ' "Quarry roughs": life and labour in Headington Quarry, 1860–1920: an essay in oral history', in R. Samuel, ed., *Village Life and Labour* (London, 1975), pp. 139–264.

Figure 6.4 Woman traveller, c. 1800. Travellers included both old and young, women as well as men. This aged female carried hardware for sale in her panniers: more common were lighter goods such as smallwares (Source: W. Pyne, *Microcosm* [London, 1806])

century became 'a long chain of villages and streets, which form one widely spread town' of 34,581 people. In other places, the bourgeoisie spread ever further from the dirt and noise of the city and transformed nearby villages into middle-class suburbs. They were typically on transport routes, often on south-facing slopes with sunny aspects and to the west of towns so the prevailing wind blew away the smell and smoke.[31]

Urbanisation not only engulfed some settlements, but also rendered others more culturally and demographically dependent. Market towns' burgeoning demand for food and their growing attractiveness for settlement brought about major changes in the culture of the villages in their hinterlands. Villagers often had relatives in the town and marriages out of the community increased. Another factor was the rise of domestic service. During the nineteenth century, the income gap between the middle and working classes increased. Before technology provided alternatives to physical labour in the provision of luxuries, these largely

31. J. Fowles and J. Draper, *Thomas Hardy's England* (London, 1984), pp. 140, 152 and 158; T. Hardy, *The Mayor of Casterbridge: The Life and Death of a Man of Character, etc.* (1886; London, 1964), pp. 254–5; Brown, 'Enclosure and improvement', pp. 138–142; N. MacMaster, 'The battle for Mousehold Heath 1857–1884: "popular politics" and the Victorian public park', *Past and Present* 127 (1990), pp. 117–54; White, *Staffordshire*, p. 681.

depended upon the employment of domestic servants. Already by 1700, Wrigley calculated that as a consequence a sixth of the population had spent a significant amount of time in London; with the growth of domestic service during the nineteenth century (rising from 11.5 per cent of the working population in 1841 to 15.4 per cent in 1881) growing numbers were aware of life beyond their village. Moreover, migration from agricultural villages also was often temporary and many returned when opportunities allowed, bringing outside ideas into the settlement.[32] (See Figure 6.4.)

Awareness of wider society through migration led to the emulation of urban behaviour which was assisted by the rise of education, sponsored largely by the church. It is true that literacy levels and access to literature was greater in the early modern period than was commonly believed, and the countryside lagged behind the towns. However the rising literacy rates and knowledge of the world produced by growing numbers of rural schools enabled the villager's imagination to travel beyond the parish's physical and social confines. Under the pressures of migration and paternalist initiatives in education, church extension and other cultural activities, traditional rural culture was being transformed by the diffusion of 'urban ideas' or, as Tonnies expressed it, the intimate 'Gemeinschaft' community of villages was being altered by the depersonalised 'Gesellschaft' society of the city or the state.[33]

The demographic changes previously outlined were intimately connected with economic forces which were already affecting village independence before 1760 and accelerated thereafter. The economic and cultural isolation of the village was eroded by increasing migration to towns, the rise of casual labour and growing numbers of itinerant sellers, originally concentrating on the homes of the rich en route to market towns but increasingly selling to the masses. Many carried chap-books which served not only to open up external economic links but also informed them of a culture beyond the parish bounds independent of the church and the

32. H. Perkin, The Origins of Modern English Society 1780–1880 (London, 1969), pp. 135–6; N. McKendrick, The Birth of Consumer Society (Bloomington, Ind., 1982), Introduction and Chapter 1; E. A. Wrigley, 'Urban growth and agricultural change: England and the continent in the early modern period', Jnl of Interdisciplinary Hist., 15 (1985), pp. 683–728; E. A. Wrigley, 'A simple model of London's importance in changing English society and economy 1650–1750', Past and Present 37 (1967), pp. 44–60; B. R. Mitchell and P. Deane, Abstract of British Historical Statistics (Cambridge, 1962), p. 196, Table 30; D. Tidswell, 'Geographical mobility, occupational changes and family relationships in early nineteenth-century Scotland' (unpublished Ph.D. thesis, Edinburgh, 1993); Pooley and Turnbull, Migration and Mobility, p. 308.
33. E. G. West, Education and the Industrial Revolution (London, 1975) p. 42; W. A. Armstrong, 'The countryside', in F. M. L. Thompson, ed., The Cambridge Social History of Britain 1750–1950, 3 vols (Cambridge, 1990), Vol. I, pp. 127–30; F. Tonnies, Community and Society: Gemeinschaft und Gesellschaft (translated and edited by C. P. Loomis) (1887; East Lansing, Michigan, 1957).

landed elite. External market forces were undermining the internal moral order imposed by the clergy.[34]

On the other hand, while villages were brought into greater economic connection with towns, this also served to isolate them by placing the links in a few hands. Village trade increasingly was carried on by intermediaries – higglers, carriers or chapmen – on behalf of fellow villagers. This was encouraged by the turnpiking of roads which made travel more expensive. After 1760, more than ever before, villages developed their own providers of goods and services to prevent the need for external ties; apart from the miller and the blacksmith, research on eighteenth-century Cheshire villages show they were also well supplied with rural craftsmen/retailers. Village stores were established even in remarkably small settlements; in Gloucestershire Compton Abdale's 130 or so inhabitants in the 1720s had no need to travel the 3½ miles to the market town of Northleach as they were served by the shop of Edward Faulkes and his wife who supplied spices, home produced honey, smallware and alum. The cheapness of their stock – only worth 28s. 2d., with a 'float' of 8s. – shows that many people could afford to set up shop. This suggests that one observer's view in 1681 that even a 'village where is (it may be) not above ten houses, there is a Shop-keeper' is not such an exaggeration as might at first appear.[35]

The rise of itinerant traders and of village stores was a double-edged sword for village independence; while they obviated the need for residents to leave the village, these retailers helped to integrate villagers both culturally and economically within the wider economy. Inventories from throughout Britain show that more prosperous villagers were already in contact with a large range of products. Evidence in court cases demonstrates that all manner of goods were obtainable from village stores. For example, three villagers stole tobacco, currants and raisins from the general stores in Sawtry All Saints (Huntingdonshire) in 1836. Even that stalwart device of the detective novel, the village store selling arsenic to murderers, had its basis in the conviction of a Norfolk villager who acquired his poison in this way.[36]

34. J. Stobart, 'The economic and social lifeworlds of rural craftsmen-retailers in eighteenth-century Cheshire', *Ag. Hist. Rev.* 52 (2004), pp. 141–60; *Times*, 10 December 1818, p. 3.

35. Gloucestershire Record Office, Diocesan Records, Inventory of Edmund Faulkes and wife, October 1731; S. Rudder, *A New History of Gloucestershire* (Cirencester, 1779); W. Carter, *The Trade of England Revived and the Abuses thereof Rectified, in Relation to Wooll and Woollen-Cloth, Silk and Silk-Weavers, Hawkers, Bankrupts, Stage-Coaches, Shop-keepers, Companies, Markets, Linnen-Cloath* (London, 1681), Section 17.

36. M. Spufford, *The Great Reclothing of Rural England: Petty Chapmen and their Wares in the Seventeenth Century* (London, 1984), pp. 107–46; L. Weatherill, *Consumer Behaviour and Material Culture in Britain 1600–1760* (London, 1988), pp. 25–42 and 191–200; Brown, *Itinerant Retailing* (forthcoming), Chapters 2, 7 and 8; Cambridgeshire Record Office, Huntingdon Quarter Sessions, HCP/1/20 (1836); *Times*, 27 May 1852, p. 7.

The role of village shops by the nineteenth century can be illustrated by a case study in Staffordshire. By using the 1851 directory, it is possible to compile a list of 218 villages which can be identified as either industrial or agricultural. Their populations, distances from market town, and the numbers of beer outlets, shops and domestic and industrial services can then be tabulated. Large industrial villages are excluded as their size would qualify them as sizeable towns. For several reasons, the distinction between retailing and domestic services is difficult to draw. For example, butchers and tailors have been counted as shopkeepers although some butchers may have been wholesaling to urban retailers and some tailors had no shop as such. Shoemakers have been considered as providers of domestic services because they sometimes had no shop front, and much of their work was repair rather than manufacture. However, some impression about the provision of retail and other services can be formed.

The research revealed that even small villages in the mid-nineteenth century had several providers of retail and domestic services. Only three of the 218 had none whatsoever – all were estate villages with an average population of just 100.[37] Industrial villages tended to be larger and were much better endowed with shops and services, especially beer outlets. Predictably the number of shops and services provided was directly proportional to the size of the settlement and its distance from a market town. Thus the economic self-containedness of villages still depended on geography and demography.

Table 6.3, which shows how many beer outlets, shops and so on were to be found on average in Staffordshire villages in 1851, reflects other trends. The first is the prevalence of beer outlets which were found even in the smallest villages but were outnumbered by shops in larger ones. The second is that the larger the village, the higher the proportion of shops and services. In short, residents could acquire most of their everyday goods and services without stirring from the village. Contemporary commentators confirm this picture; in Black Country industrial villages in 1869, 'People did not move very far from home to shop. They bought shoes and ironmongery from cheap jack travelling vans and food and clothing from "Tommy shops"'. This situation applied elsewhere; in 1885, Willington colliery village in Durham 'has its own shops, where all can be obtained that the miner is likely to require'.[38] Nevertheless, villagers were being integrated slowly and inexorably into the wider economy. Although some goods originated locally, most were produced elsewhere.

A local approach also shows that the rise of industrial society after 1760 did not

37. Patshull (117), Ingestre (118) and Oakover (67).
38. *Times*, 15 August 1885, p. 7 col. a; A. Payne, *Pits and Furnaces or Life in the Black Country* (London, 1869).

Table 6.3 Summary statistics of shops and services in 218 Staffordshire villages in 1851

	Beer outlets	Shops	'Domestic services'	'Industrial services'	Total
Total	799	1069	695	904	3467
Mean per village	3.7	4.9	3.2	4.1	15.9
Mode per village	2	1	1	2	7
Median per village	2	3	2	3	10

Source: White's *Staffordshire Directory* (1851).

have the same economic impact upon all communities. One reason for this is the huge variety of village types with differing levels of independence and self-sufficiency. For example, a northern Pennine village was so distant from markets that residents only occasionally reached a town and depended a good deal on the most determined itinerant traders; until the arrival of improved transport, wider economic change made little impact. Another reason is the accident of local economic development. Improvements in local arable farming allowed the traditional culture associated with the hiring fair in the East Riding to survive unusually in the period 1850–75.[39] The accident of new transport systems, produced by entrepreneurial adventure and economic dictates, had an enormous effect. A guide book of 1900 noted that 'Ickenham is situated off the beaten track and far from the encroachment of any railway. Ickenham village changes little year to year and remains one of the most rural of our Middlesex villages'. Its isolation was mainly because no major road passed through it despite its nearness to London. However when two railways arrived in 1905, followed by the underground, the village rapidly transformed into a suburb of Uxbridge.[40] The presence and awareness of workable minerals transformed existing villages like Millom in Cumberland which had 79 households in 1851 with 409 inhabitants, virtually all working in agriculture. After the haematite mine opened in 1855, a new settlement expanded on the edge of the village and the population expanded rapidly; in 1871 there were 479 households and 2,656 inhabitants. In the words of the 1901 directory: 'The old village, around which was shed a halo of antiquity, has lost much of its individuality, and now presents the appearance of a respectable suburb to New Town'.[41]

Apart from transforming existing communities, economic change created new

39. G. Moses, 'Reshaping rural culture? The Church of England and hiring fairs in the East Riding of Yorkshire *c.* 1850–80', *Rural Hist.* 13 (2002), pp. 61–84.
40. *VCH Middlesex*, Vol. IV, pp. 100–2.
41. T. Bulmer, *History & Directory of Cumberland* (Preston, 1901), sub Millom; A. Harris, 'Millom: a Victorian new town,' *Trans. Cumberland and Westmorland Antiq. and Arch. Soc.* 66 (1966), pp. 449–67; Millom census returns 1851 and 1871.

groups of settlements including textile colonies, industrial villages and urban villages. As towns and cities expanded, they too acquired urban villages like Haggerstone in London. With increasing residential segregation, they were often the poor parts of town and so attracted the poorest newcomers – in the nineteenth century this was often the Irish. As Lees wrote, such urban villages were 'more a cultural than a physical community'. While some were united by attracting specific groups of migrants, others were united by the fact that they had a single owner, an employer who wanted his workforce to live near his factory. Many of these were 'textile colonies' which were numerous and had a strong inward sense of community like Ashton's Flowery Field colony adjoining Hyde (Cheshire), where the inhabitants had some sense of loyalty to the owner. Other urban villages were deliberately planned as model communities like Shaftesbury Park near Clapham (Surrey), in which artisans were provided with a reading room, lecture theatre, cooperative stores, schools, baths, washhouses, play and cricket grounds. However it was not wholly self-contained – a railway was included for commuters. Unfortunately the plan ended in increased rents and accusations of fraud. Some sociologists claimed that relatively stable urban villages survived until slum clearance after 1945; however these villages were certainly also integrated into the wider urban and indeed national community through cultural, demographic and political forces.[42]

Rural industrial villages which proliferated after 1760 also had elements of self-containedness. Whatever the actual rates of inward or outward mobility and re-migration, many factors served to retain settlers. Such villages often developed in remote areas which were necessarily isolated and originally were connected with the outside world largely through itinerants attracted by the market opportunities among these captive customers. Gradually shops and other services were established which further reduced the need for inhabitants to leave the community.[43] However the goods and raw materials produced in such settlements, and the transport systems which developed to exploit them, integrated the villages within a larger economy. Railways, which carried away goods and minerals, also brought both nationally branded goods to supply the village shops and sellers of services like the 'industrial insurance' salesman dealing with working people in competition with the more locally based friendly societies.

42. L. H. Lees, *Exiles of Erin: Irish Migrants in Victorian London* (Manchester, 1979), p. 87; B Trinder, 'Industrial towns 1700–1840', in P. Clark, ed., *The Cambridge Urban History of Britain II 1540–1840* (Cambridge, 2000), pp. 805–30; *Times*, 16 October 1873, p. 10 col. b; *Times*, 7 May 1877, p. 6 col. f and 26 Jul. 1877, p. 12 col. a; L. Mumford, 'The neighbourhoods and the neighbourhood unit', *Town Planning Rev.* 24 (1954), pp. 256–70.
43. J. Benson, *British Coalminers in the Nineteenth Century: A Social History* (London, 1989).

There were other economic factors which firmly bound industrial communities together. In some instances, especially where the village was built by an employer, its residents shared a common workplace. The prevalence of poverty, illness and death promoted communal self help and the development of cultural communities.[44] In the mining industry particularly, the shared danger of the work bred a particular type of tight-knit community. In the Black Country, the death rate in coal mines was 8:1000 in the 1850s which, when the normal working life of a miner – say thirty years – is considered, meant that perhaps a quarter of all miners died underground while an equal number at least were maimed.[45] Indeed the growth of unions and of cartels of mine owners eroded mining villages' independence; disputes would often involve miners from several places. Thus in 1869, 2,000 people from several local villages assembled in Mold in Flintshire to riot after their union leaders were sentenced to a month's imprisonment, and soldiers shot five dead. This echoed the collective behaviour of miners from different villages on many occasions in the nineteenth century. In the north-east, although mining communities were notoriously inward-looking, 70,000 miners gathered in Durham for their annual festival in 1885.[46] The settlements often developed a culture which encouraged communal introspection; leisure activities like dominoes, darts, quoits, football, whippet racing and pigeon fancying were pursuable largely without leaving the village. Indeed public houses provided facilities for these leisure pursuits for commercial reasons. In Willington (County Durham), 'the miners, being in the habit of making their own amusements, have, when in work, but little time or inducement to stray far from the precincts of their little kingdom'. Often there was a place of worship – typically nonconformist – which was shared by most of the workers. However the rise of dissent, like the rise of shops, placed all village communities literally within a larger circuit. The success of Methodism depended not only on its message but also its adaptable organisation; groups of worshippers over a district started by meeting in houses, barns or even the open air, with ministers servicing the needs of a whole district and worshippers travelling to services outside their parish. Even Anglicans travelled to hear better preachers despite the efforts of landlords like Sir John Boileau of Ketteringham in Norfolk who closed his park to prevent such journeys. This brought worshippers into communion with those of other villages.[47]

44. J. Benson, *The Working Class in Britain 1850–1939* (London, 1989).
45. G. Barnsby, *Social Conditions in the Black Country* (Wolverhampton, 1980), p. 31.
46. *Times*, 4 June 1869, p. 12, 10 January 1831, p. 3 col. e and 15 August 1885, p. 7 col. a.
47. A. D. Gilbert, *Religion and Society in Industrial England: Church, Chapel and Social Change, 1740–1914* (London, 1976), pp. 21, 53–7; *Times*, 15 August 1885, p. 7 col. a; O. Chadwick, *Victorian Miniature*, 2nd edn (London, 1983), pp. 49 and 82.

Table 6.4 The impact of truck in Monmouthshire, 1830

Item	Market shop	Company shop	Mark up
Flour (per pack)	2s. 4d.	2s. 6d.	2d.
Bacon (4 lb)	2s. 0d.	3s. 0d.	1s. 0d.
Mutton (2 lb)	10d.	1s. 0d.	2d.
Beef (2 lb)	8d.	11d.	3d.
Sugar (1 lb)	8d.	9d.	1d.
Butter (1 lb)	9d.	1s. 0d.	3d.
Tea (2 oz)	8d.	1s. 0d.	4d.
Cheese (2 lb)	1s. 0d.	1s. 6d.	6d.
Total	8s.11d.	11s. 8d.	2s. 9d.

Source: *Monmouthshire Merlin,* March 1830.

Some employers saw advantages in creating self-contained settlements. Cromford's site in Derbyshire was chosen not only because of its reliable water power but also it lay at some distance from potential machine breakers. Its isolation obliged Arkwright to establish a market and an inn. Other employers copied his example and while factory villages and colonies had a high turnover originally, they gradually gained stability and employers saw several economic advantages in retaining the village's separation.[48]

One was the opportunity to profit from the sale of goods to the residents at 'tommy shops'. Workers were often paid in tokens or truck which could only be spent in factory shops on overpriced items. Although outlawed in 1831, the practice persisted over the next forty years at least in the industrial villages of the Black Country. Workers voicing complaints were blacklisted by employers, who were often the magistrates who enforced the law.[49] Workers sometimes organised themselves to protest and even riot,[50] but others were complicit in the system because they could get instantaneous payment and in 1868 over half of the Black Country's hand-made nails were willingly exchanged for truck.[51] Moreover truck was also paid in agricultural villages, but this was much rarer than in industrial areas.[52] Truck restricted the economic independence of the workers by obliging them to buy most of their goods within the community and to pay as much as a 29 per cent mark up, as Table 6.4 illustrates.

Apart from truck, company-owned shops and cottages brought other advantages to the employer by keeping workers in their jobs. Credit and rent

48. A. Redford, *Labour Migration in England 1800–1850* (Manchester, 1926), pp. 20–30.
49. 1 and 2 William IV. c. xxxvii; D. Philips, *Crime and Authority in Victorian England: The Black Country 1835–1860* (London, 1975); SRO, Hatherton Papers D260/M/F/5/18.
50. *Times*, 10 January 1831, p. 3 col. e.
51. E. Burritt, *Walks in the Black Country and its Green Borderland* (London, 1868), p. 122.
52. *Times*, 25 December 1846, 'The peasantry in the South of England'.

arrears reinforced self-containedness. Changing jobs meant more disruption because it involved leaving the village. Further there was usually work for children in the local industry and the resultant continuity of employment tended to bind them as adults into their native community.[53]

Many of these employers' settlements were new foundations which gave the owner the opportunity of controlling access to the settlement and so render them more self-contained. Often tollgates were placed across their sole access roads to limit access from outside traders and were sometimes closed in the evening.[54] On the fuzzy margins between profit and philanthropy, many factory owners also provided employees with recreational opportunities both to avoid them taking up political or immoral activities and to make them associate more closely with the firm and incidentally the community. They based their choice of activities on the interests of the workers themselves, establishing brass bands, sporting facilities or working men's clubs. Many north-eastern colliery companies provided literary institutes in their pit villages for similar reasons.[55] Some collieries even provided hospitals for their workers.[56]

Some industrialists, inspired by philanthropy and ideas of improvement, went further and founded self-contained settlements containing good quality dwellings of adequate size, with proper facilities for their workers including schools and cooperative shops. In these cases the fourth criterion outlined at the beginning, the cultural changes in the village, become particularly clear. Developing out of late eighteenth-century factory settlements like Mellor (Derbyshire), Cromford (Derbyshire) and New Lanark, and influenced perhaps by self-contained Moravian settlements like Fairfield (Derbyshire), these villages proliferated during the nineteenth century. A few were bolted on to existing settlements like Belper in Derbyshire; others evolved gradually, with amenities added as the owners gained the means.[57] Thomas Bazley and Robert Gardner built the industrial village at Barrow Bridge near Bolton from 1826. Apart from the quality of the cottages, its evolving institutions made it a model self-contained settlement. For example, from 1836 it had a cooperative shop managed by a committee of workmen. The village school was open to the children of all residents including those who were not employees. Other villages were built and designed from the outset as model settlements like Nenthead (Cumberland) built for 1500 lead miners in the

53. *Times*, 31 December 1870, p. 10 col. a.
54. G. T. Gray, *Witton Park: its Past and Present* (place unstated, 1903).
55. *Times*, 15 August 1885, p. 7 col. a.
56. *Times*, 6 September 1870, p. 8 col. f.
57. E. G. Power, *A Textile Community in the Industrial Revolution* (Harlow, 1969); A. Ure, *Philosophy of Manufactures*, 3rd edn (London, 1861), pp. 342–3; N. Gordon, 'Blantyre', in D. Burns, A. Reid and I. Walker, eds, *Hamilton District: A History* (Hamilton, 1995).

Pennines by a firm dominated by benevolent Quakers. Its excellent facilities including public baths, a washhouse and allotments, and physical isolation meant that a close knit community evolved.[58]

Mining and factory villages built by philanthropists aimed to provide for all of the needs of the villagers as part of a programme of shaping the moral character of the workers. Substitutes for public houses like playing fields, allotment gardens and libraries were often provided. They reflected the philanthropist's moral agenda; thus John Grubb Richardson ensured that Bessbrook in Antrim was without the four p's – pub, poverty, pawnshop and police station – but had a dispensary, savings bank, village hall, churches and shops. Even the common character of its architecture gave villages like Reckitt's Garden Village in Hull an intangible element of self-containedness. Peter Gaskell in 1836 commended model manufacturing villages like Styal as 'one great family bound together by common ties and dependent on one common master'. While there were more of these settlements than the usual brief list cited – New Lanark, Saltaire (Yorkshire), Port Sunlight (Cheshire) and Bournville (in Birmingham) were joined by the less famous Egerton (Cheshire), Halliwell (Lancashire), Ironville and Cressbrook (both Derbyshire) and Akroydon, Copley, New Earswick, Sharlston, Birstwith (all Yorkshire) – relatively few people lived in them.[59]

Industrial and commercial profits also sustained another type of self-contained village. Many philanthropists sought to establish themselves as a sort of urban aristocracy with an industrial rather than an agricultural estate and gained status through the approbation of their contemporaries. Thus Disraeli based his ideal factory owner Mr Millbank in his novel *Coningsby* on the work of Thomas Bazley and Robert Gardner at Barrow Bridge which he had seen four years before. Millbank created a factory village, providing a church, a clerical residence, a schoolhouse and an institute. No wonder Prince Albert visited Barrow Bridge and Bazley ended up a baronet with a model estate at Hatherop.[60] Similarly when *The Times* reported on the model colliery village of Bolsover 'such as one is accustomed to see clustering around the park gateways of some wealthy and public spirited landed proprietor' it mentioned its chief proprietor, Emerson Bainbridge MP.[61] However like the Bazleys and the Bainbridges (who also created the model agricultural village of Esholt in Northumberland around their improved mansion), some still sought to use their industrial and commercial profits to acquire and

58. *Times*, 13 October 1851, p. 4 col. d.
59. Hull University, Brynmor Jones Library, Records of Isaac Reckitt (DRA/618–629); Peter Gaskell, *Artisans and Machinery* (London, 1836), pp. 89–91.
60. W. E. A. Axon, ed., *The Annals of Manchester* (Manchester, 1886), 22 January 1876.
61. *Times*, 19 November 1896, p. 8 col. a.

shape their own self-contained aristocratic communities, aping the Lord Harcourt at Nuneham Courtenay, the Duke of Devonshire at Edensor or the Prince of Wales at Sandringham.[62] These were usually aesthetically pleasing but increasingly incorporated more facilities than the obligatory church.[63] The choice of amenities again reflected the whims of the individual owner; most prohibited public houses; others also included institutions to benefit the community like health insurance for estate workers which bound them into the estate. Some employed new technology – sometimes reservoirs were built and in one late example even an electricity supply and a bathing pool.[64] In the nineteenth century, as previously, the number of such owner-dominated model settlements constituted a tiny minority. However these examples show that industrial society, far from ending aristocratic model villages, provided the wherewithal for their continuance into the twentieth century.

Certainly there was a desire amongst some members of all classes to resist the onset of urbanisation and to support the principle of self-contained villages, combining the best of the countryside and the town. This insight is usually associated with Ebenezer Howard and the garden city movement in the early twentieth century which envisaged self-contained settlements, albeit larger than industrial villages. However similar initiatives pre-dated his – Lowell's industrial villages in the north-east of the USA, Owenite communities, Chartist settlements, the Allotment Movement, the Society for Promoting Industrial Villages and settlements established by the Salvation Army, the Co-operative Movement and philanthropic industrialists. All in one way or another sought to recreate mythical, self-contained rural communities. The Society for Promoting Industrial Villages was founded in 1884 'to ascertain the best means of establishing villages where manufactures and 'home industries' can be combined with the cultivation of cottage, or cooperative farms, as a remedy for over-crowding in great cities and want of employment in agricultural districts'. At a conference about the project, several speakers argued that industrial settlements would not acquire the moral

62. M. Batey, 'Nuneham Courtenay: an Oxfordshire eighteenth-century deserted village', *Oxoniensia* 33 (1968), pp. 108–24; *Times*, 28 December 1891, p. 4 col. e and 27 December 1871.
63. *Times*, 10 July 1846, p. 5 col. d, 'Condition of the peasantry in Dorsetshire' and 11 November 1848, p. 8 col. e; Milton Abbas Museum; B. Bramsen and K. Wain, *The Hambros 1779–1979* (London, 1979), pp. 109–10, 251, 258 and 337–44; *Times*, 9 December 1885, p. 11 col. f and 2 October 1885, p. 10 col. e; G. Battiscombe, *Shaftesbury* (London, 1974), pp. 168–9, 260–1 and 326; R. C. on *Housing the Working Class* (P. P. 1884–5, 30), p. 537; J. W. Day, 'The squire of Newmarket', *Country Life* 113 (1953), pp. 1066–7; *Times*, 27 December 1893, p. 5 col. d.
64. E. C. Brooks, *Sir Morton Peto Bart* (Bury St Edmunds, 1996), pp. 46–7; Warwickshire Record Office (hereafter WaRO), Dugdale Mss. 313/1 17. 6. 1848; *Times*, 16 November 1908, p. 13; *Tamworth Herald*, 7 January 1882, p. 5 col. 4; WaRO, CR 456 Box 8; E. A. B. Barnard, *Stanton, Snowshill, Gloucestershire* (Cambridge, 1927).

character of the traditional village and instanced existing new industrial settlements which had grown into towns like Wolverton (Buckinghamshire) and Swindon (Wiltshire). However the real problem with this and other similar schemes was that industrialists found that domestic industry could not compete with goods produced by mechanisation.[65]

The definition of the self-contained village evolved with the rise of industrial society; a correspondent to *The Times* in 1893 complained that his village was threatened with partition between two parishes when it had 'all the characteristics of a real independent village community ... a church, endowed school, infant school, reading room, public house, water supply, allotments, post office, cricket ground, [and] library'. Such a list, reflecting not only technological change but also increased expectations produced by the social transformation of the previous century and a half, was very different to any example produced at the start of this period.[66]

To conclude, despite regional variations,[67] the rise of industrial society after 1760 tended to reduce what remained of the cultural 'self-containedness' of villages. In administrative terms, new and extra-parochial settlements were regimented into parishes with councils, resident clergy and schools. They were suborned into poor law unions and policed by county forces. Demographically, villages near towns were either swallowed up or transformed by the inflow of urban commuters. Migration between towns and countryside was commonplace.

In economic terms, this chapter has shown that the rise of industrial society brought about conflicting change. In some ways, the self-sufficiency of villages actually increased. Many Staffordshire villages in 1851 could satisfy the everyday needs of the residents. Some of the new industrial villages were self-contained through the nature of the work and the deliberate policy of the employers. However, the rise of industrial society also eroded the independence of villages. The demand for foodstuffs from growing towns encouraged the adoption of new farming methods to create surpluses which increasingly integrated villages within a regional economy, dominated by towns. Systems of cheap and rapid transportation of both goods and passengers encouraged integration into the wider world.

Perhaps more insidiously, the ideology of free market capitalism permeated villages and broke down their cultural isolation. Despite the schemes of both

65. H. Rider Haggard, *Rural England* (London, 1902); DNB, sub George Herring 1832–1906; *Times*, 24 December 1884, p. 8 and 27 June 1885, p. 11 col. c.
66. *Times*, 8 November 1893, p. 14 cols b-c. An example of how expectations continued to change is given by Barlaston Garden Village created by the Wedgwood Pottery Company from 1934: *Times*, 12 September 1938, p. 8 col. d.
67. A. Howkins, *Reshaping Rural England: a Social History 1850–1925* (London, 1991).

radicals and paternalists, the inexorable success of the free market meant that few model villages were actually built or prospered and what George Bourne called the 'customary system' in villages had been marginalised by 1912.[68] Village societies have gradually converged into rural society, which in turn has been altered – but as the recent appearance of the Countryside Alliance demonstrates, not overwhelmed – by urban-dominated society.[69]

68. G. Bourne, *Change in the Village* (London, 1912), p. 93.
69. For a description of how even a fairly remote Cambridgeshire village in the twentieth century has been culturally overwhelmed by urban influence, see R. Page, *The Decline of an English Village* (Shedfield, 1989).

Conclusion

CHRISTOPHER DYER

As has been recalled by a number of the contributors to this book, its starting point in historical writing lay in the revelation in the 1960s that villagers moved constantly, and that the countryside was not full of stay-at-home peasants, whose family were long rooted in the same place. These essays have not challenged that not-so-new orthodoxy, but they are written in the post-Laslett age. We have now all recovered from the shock of his discovery, and can begin to assess the wider significance of a mobile population for our assessment of rural society.

The first point to make is the lack of local uniformity, as everyone agrees that in the pre-industrial period the rate of migration in and out of villages and the consequent discontinuity in family succession varied from place to place. In general eastern England and particularly East Anglia and Essex experienced a higher rate of population turnover than other parts of the country. This reflects such variables as the commercial pressures on the countryside, the development of the land market, and the power of lordship. More local contrasts of landscape and society, such as the distinctions between woodland and champion in the midlands, suggest the paradox that the woodlands, supposedly more fluid and dynamic, retained families longer than the champion villages which were famed for their conservatism and stability. Proximity to a large town might encourage a village's population to stay.

The second qualification refers to the changing pace of movement, which may have been lower in the period before the Black Death, and reached a peak in the fifteenth century when the inheritance of holdings in many villages became something of a rarity. The rate of migration may sometimes have slowed in the sixteenth century, though a great deal of movement is recorded in the seventeenth and eighteenth centuries. One factor here was demographic, as people with land were more reluctant to move if the demand for land was high.

The third reservation is to point out the variety of behaviour depending on social rank and age. Young servants moved more than anyone, many of them females. Smallholders and labourers were especially prone to migrate. Those involved in the rural cloth industry saw opportunities elsewhere and moved frequently. Clearly the search for employment (or better employment) was a major incentive for people to move. At the other end of the scale of wealth, calculations of profit may have persuaded landholders, especially the most substantial farmers, to sell up and establish themselves in a more advantageous place, and the gentry were even more likely to uproot and seek an heiress or a new estate at a distance. On the other hand, better-off families, who tended to fill the official positions in manor court or vestry, had a stronger motive to stay. Some of these in Cumbria and elsewhere combined landholding with some steady craft or trade, such as working as wheelwright or smith. One can see stable individuals, like Richard Gough of Myddle, or the Wylmott family of Hartlebury, or the Bisshops of Hevingham Bishops who could survey the constant departures and arrivals among their neighbours, and provided some element of continuity in the midst of migration. These families were not entirely confined within their parishes, for example by choosing marriage partners from outside. Over a long period the pattern of migration had common characteristics. Most people went to rural rather than urban destinations, and the great majority of movements fell within a limit of 20 miles. Behind the generalisation that much migration took place, many variations have to be appreciated. There is much that is still not understood: for example, a high turnover of families in a locality is regarded by some historians as evidence of vitality, while others see it as a sign of decay.

Having accepted that migration, though varied, was a commonplace, some contributors point out that this was not necessarily damaging to the villagers' identity and sense of belonging. In most villages, as we have seen, a few families provided links with the past. Customs and traditions were not so ancient, and a collective memory going back two generations was enough to give the inhabitants a feeling for the special character of their village. In any case, rural society was constantly changing, and new methods and skills could be acquired from the newcomers. The migrants went through a process of assimilation, in which they absorbed the ways of the village, and if of the right class and character, were accepted into the elite of elders and officeholders.

This process by which migrants were drawn into the community helps to explain the strong identification with a particular place which was clearly felt by villagers, and which found expression in a writer such as Gough, who used the possession of pews in the parish church as the framework of his account of village society. The administration of the poor law after 1598 reveals the ambiguities of parochial loyalty. On the one hand the leaders of village society became conscious of the parish boundary and collective space such as the church porch as never before, but on the other they were faced with the difficulty of defining who exactly belonged to the parish. They had to confront the reality of constant migration with an unrealistic ideal that each parish contained a fixed body of residents with a right to claim poor relief.

Laslett's generalisation about early modern mobility, together with the parallel thinking about the Middle Ages, helped to undermine the idea that villages began as self-sufficient and stable societies, which then lost their innocence under the pressures of modern society and government. The poor law of the sixteenth and seventeenth centuries imposed new responsibilities on to the parish. Now the parishioners had to define their territory and its inhabitants with minute precision, and collect money from the better-off inhabitants in greater quantities than ever before. On the one hand the state was intruding into the heart of village society and government by imposing a poor law, but on the other hand it strengthened village self-government and villagers' attachment to their community as a by-product of administering poor relief.

In the same way the enclosure movement, as it affected villages in Cumbria, did not take away common assets and immediately polarise society between the yeomen and the labourers. Rather it strengthened the economic position of the middling ranks of landed society, who worked their holdings with family and servant labour. The labourers had lost their common rights long before, so they were not disadvantaged by the enclosure of the common waste. The traditional Cumbrian village with its peasant farming survived into the eighteenth century and even later.

Market forces are often seen in their constant expansion as a threat to the economic autonomy of the village. Current thinking makes the story more complicated, as market forces are regarded as a powerful influence on rural society well before 1300, and peasants are seen as heavily engaged in selling produce, consuming manufactured and traded goods, and buying and selling land. In the long run the market encouraged agricultural specialisation, which put new pressure on village fields, and further promoted inequality among the inhabitants. In the eighteenth and early nineteenth centuries, however, the industrial revolution, far from killing off self-sufficiency, helped to create new villages inhabited by industrial workers or retail traders. There was even a need for a new generation of parish churches to be built in the industrial districts. The village shop enabled the inhabitants to obtain their necessities on their doorstep, rather than having to visit a market town. Horizons broadened in the sense that people bought more goods, including imported commodities such as tea, but they narrowed in that they no longer travelled to make their purchases.

It is often said that the outlook of country people was transformed by the arrival of education, written matter and easier communications. Cheap print, such as chap-books, possibly broadened minds, but as we have seen late medieval peasants dependent on oral transmission knew a good deal about national politics. We are reminded that the turnpiking of roads increased the cost of travel, and restriction of common rights meant that cottagers who might have owned a horse in the fifteenth century, had to walk in the eighteenth, so perhaps the poor did not see their chances for travel increase.

The village which lived on its own resources and kept itself in isolation is a myth which has its roots in a romantic nostalgia for a wholesome rural past that never existed, and in historical notions that society progressed in a continuous linear path from simple communities to the complexities of modern life. Country people, from the earliest records available, were always in touch with the outside world through migration, trade, government, religion and ideas. In certain places and times, however, the external contacts of villagers were strengthened as the state made greater demands, and the commercial economy intensified. Sometimes the pace of change was slow, and even went into reverse, as the administration of the poor law, or the arrival of the village shop, could make rural economies seem more autonomous. The self-contained village probably never existed, and was certainly not in continuous decline between 1250 and 1900.

Index

LIST OF OCCASIONAL PAPERS
DEPARTMENT OF ENGLISH LOCAL HISTORY,
UNIVERSITY OF LEICESTER

4.   Alan Everitt, *The Pattern of Rural Dissent: the Nineteenth Century* (1972)
5.   David Hey, *The Rural Metalworkers of the Sheffield Region* (1972)
6.   Cyril Hart, *The Hidation of Cambridgeshire* (1974)

Third Series
1.   J. S. Morrill, *The Cheshire Grand Jury 1625–1659* (1976)
2.   Katherine S. Naughton, *The Gentry of Bedfordshire in the Thirteenth and Fourteenth Centuries* (1976)
3.   Prudence Ann Moylan, *The Form and Reform of County Government: Kent 1889–1914* (1978)
4.   Charles Phythian-Adams, *Continuity, Fields and Fission: the Making of a Midland Parish* (1978)
5.   B. J. Davey, *Ashwell, 1830–1914: the Decline of a Village Community* (1980)
6.   Beryl Schumer, *The Evolution of Wychwood to 1400: Pioneers, Frontiers and Forests* (1984)

Fourth Series
1.   Charles Phythian-Adams, *Re-thinking English Local History* (1987)
2.   Peter Warner, *Greens, Commons and Clayland Colonization: the Origins and Development of Green-side Settlement in East Suffolk* (1987)
3.   K. D. M. Snell, *Church and Chapel in the North Midlands: Religious Observance in the Nineteenth Century* (1991)
4.   Christopher Dyer, *Hanbury: Settlement and Society in a Woodland Landscape* (1991)

Associated Volumes
1.   Charles Phythian-Adams (ed.), *Societies, Cultures and Kinship, 1580–1850: Cultural Provinces and English Local History*, with contributions by Mary Carter, Evelyn Lord and Anne Mitson (1993)
2.   Harold Fox, *The Evolution of the Fishing Village: Landscape and Society along the South Devon Coast, 1086-1550*, Leicester Explorations in Local History Volume I (Leopard's Head Press, Oxford, 2001)

Note
Virtually all of the Occasional Papers listed above are out of print. Third Series number 6, by Beryl Schumer, has been republished by The Wychwood Press (Jon Carpenter Publishing), Charlbury, Oxfordshire. *The Evolution of the Fishing Village* may be obtained by writing to 'Explorations', Centre for English Local History, 5 Salisbury Road, Leicester LE1 7QR.